Until the Last One's Found

Until the Last One's Found

An Introduction to
Universal Reconciliation
and Restoration

CURT PARTON

WIPF & STOCK · Eugene, Oregon

UNTIL THE LAST ONE'S FOUND
An Introduction to Universal Reconciliation and Restoration

Wipf & Stock
An Imprint of Wipf and Stock Publishers
199 W. 8th Ave., Suite 3
Eugene, OR 97401

www.wipfandstock.com

PAPERBACK ISBN: 979-8-3852-2543-9
HARDCOVER ISBN: 979-8-3852-2544-6
EBOOK ISBN: 979-8-3852-2545-3

VERSION NUMBER 07/18/24

For my wife, Kelley,

and for my church family
who are living this story with me

Suppose one of you has a hundred sheep and loses one of them.
Doesn't he leave the ninety-nine in the open country
and go after the lost sheep until he finds it?

LUKE 15:4

Contents

First Things First

Chapter One

Introductions

WHEN YOU PICK UP a book such as this, it's natural to wonder: *Who is this person? And why are they writing this?* So, let me start by telling a little about me, then you'll have some idea who the author is as you're reading this book. I'm a fairly ordinary evangelical pastor. (I'm using "evangelical" in a theological sense of the word not in a cultural or political one.) Most would consider me a theologically conservative evangelical. I whole-heartedly affirm biblical, historical, orthodox Christianity. I believe strongly that—because he is God who came to us as one of us—the way Jesus Christ has provided for us to be reconciled to God is the *only* way we can be reconciled to God. I believe in the profound truth of substitutionary atonement or, more simply put, that Christ died in our place, taking on the consequences of our sin. He took on our death so we can receive his life.

In today's cultural climate, some would likely consider me too conservative and others not conservative enough. For example, I advocate a firm commitment to biblical inerrancy, but I don't condemn those who are committed to the authority of Scripture but describe that commitment differently. As long as we share a devotion to Christ as divine Lord and Savior, seek to hear the voices of other Christians over the last two millennia, and make our final appeals on the ground of Scripture—seeking together to understand it faithfully—then I would see a basis for discussion as brothers and sisters, fellow followers of Christ.

I'm not writing as a scholar, and I make no claim to be one. (Full disclosure: My pastoral training was in the form of church-based theological education, of which I remain a strong proponent.) There are wonderful books that have been written delving into the philosophy, hermeneutics, theology, and history of Christian universalism. I'm not seeking to replicate these efforts, even if I could. I've been a pastor for twenty-seven years, and the concerns motivating me to write this book are more narrowly pastoral in nature. My intention is to provide a logical and systematic introduction to this view, but one that's very accessible and easy to follow for those who don't routinely read books on theology or philosophy. I would hope this book can still be edifying for the more scholarly among us, but I'm primarily writing to everyday pastors, church leaders, and interested Christians. I've tried to make these concepts as simple and understandable as possible—but, as a teacher, it won't break my heart if you have to reach for a dictionary once or twice while reading this!

I'm a pastor, but I'm an ordinary pastor. I don't serve a megachurch, and mine isn't a familiar name in evangelicaldom. I'm neither particularly traditional nor iconoclastic (anti-tradition). The church I serve (The Orchard in Fair Oaks, California) would be considered traditional in some ways and quite nontraditional in others. We don't have a senior or lead pastor but are led by a team of pastoral elders. Our main weekly gatherings are largely dedicated to expositional study of Scripture, which we work through in context, book by book, chapter by chapter, paragraph by paragraph. But these biblical studies are always interactive; the people actually respond to questions from the one teaching, and they raise their hands and ask questions when something is unclear to them. Because of the interactive nature of our weekly studies they typically run over an hour (and it's not uncommon for people to have even more questions to discuss after the service ends). The music in our services is intended to help us focus on God in simple, heartfelt, corporate worship rather than highlighting the performance of our musicians. We meet on Sunday evenings, and enjoy a meal together each week, and our meeting space looks more like a large living room than a typical church sanctuary.

You would probably find some facets of our church life very familiar, and other aspects would likely strike you as unusual. We strive for everything we are and do to be rooted in, centered on, and permeated by the gospel of Jesus Christ. We don't seek innovation for the sake of innovation, but we've been willing to change any of our church practices to make us more faithful to what we understand to be our biblical mission as a church. We're *willing* to change, but not *seeking* change. And this ministry context tells you something about me. I don't feel locked into traditional views; I don't have a problem with considering a nontraditional perspective (especially one that enjoys a rich heritage in broader church history). But I'm also not seeking theological novelty for the sake of theological novelty.

If you had told me the first book I would write would be on the subject of "evangelical universalism," I would never have believed you! How did I come to write on *this* topic?! It wasn't because I was seeking out some strange new view, that's for sure! When, a few years ago, a good friend shared with me he was a "Christian universalist," my first thought (unexpressed) was: *"I don't think you can be that!"* He gave me a couple of books to read, and I wasn't overly impressed at the time. But the idea was then on my radar, and I had at least a theological curiosity.

I won't go through the details of my story, but I continued to periodically encounter various books on the nature of hell in general and on universal reconciliation in particular. (I'll list some of the works I found especially compelling at the end of this book.) This exposure to a thoroughly evangelical form of universalism happened somewhat in waves, over time, with each succeeding wave causing me to think more seriously about these ideas. In late 2017, I was teaching a leadership training class for our church, and they wanted to take a detour to better understand both Calvinism and Arminianism. I had been doing some more reading at that time on Christian universalism—reading I found to be increasingly compelling—but I had no desire to introduce to this church group any new ideas about hell or judgment. Quite the opposite, I was very careful to not even *mention* the subject! But as our last discussion in this detour on Calvinism ended, out of the blue, someone asked about universalism. I answered briefly about the differing views of hell that evangelical Christians hold. The people were interested in understanding these different views of hell and why evangelicals believe them, so we took *another* detour to examine the various understandings of hell. (I'll describe these differing views in the next chapter.)

Whenever I lead these kinds of studies comparing different theological views, I seek to present each view as effectively as I can, as if it were my own. This is especially fun when the people I'm teaching don't know what my personal view actually is. If they can't figure out which position I hold, I feel I'm presenting everything fairly. Each week, the people in this leadership class were convinced *this* was my view (whatever view we were studying that night). When we came to the end of the study, they were eager to learn which understanding of hell I actually believed. I openly shared with them I was still working through that question myself, and that I was finding it difficult to refute the evangelical universalism view. I invited them to continue studying and to share with me anything they thought might counter a belief in universal reconciliation and restoration. The people responded personally to this new (to us) belief—and to just the existence of alternative Christian beliefs—with varying degrees of interest and resistance. But all agreed this wasn't something we needed to be dogmatic about, and that sincere Christians could hold to any of these views.

Moving forward, the members of our leadership team would occasionally discuss the question of hell, but the subject was mostly on the back burner as we focused on other developments in our church. I continued to study the subject in my spare time, seeking to be diligent to dot all the i's and cross all the t's biblically and theologically. But I never brought up the issue or any alternative views in my regular teaching to the whole church. In the fall of 2020, we were asking for topics any of our people wanted to cover in a weekly study and discussion group we offered. Our policy for this group was that we would study and discuss *anything* that anyone wanted to study and discuss. As you can now guess, one of the topics that people wanted to study and discuss was hell and the different views on hell. Again, the responses to the differing views varied greatly, but there was strong consensus that people in our church should have the freedom to hold any of these three views.

This open church study understandably led to more conversations within our church. Eventually we discussed the issue as a congregation and decided—unanimously—that we would officially provide the freedom for anyone in our church, including pastors and leaders, to hold and teach differing views regarding hell. I began receiving requests for a simple, easy to understand explanation of the universal reconciliation and restoration view, so I wrote a twelve-post blog series to provide an accessible but systematic introduction to these ideas. This blog series led to more discussions, and many who read the series encouraged me to publish these posts as a book. What you're reading now is the culmination of these studies, the blog series, and these subsequent discussions.

You may have heard the expression the church should be *"reformed and always reforming."* What continually reforms us isn't church tradition, no matter how familiar or beloved, and it's not cultural development, no matter how personally compelling it may be. What reforms the people of God is the Spirit of God continually drawing us back to the Word of God. In his excellent introduction to the second edition of *Four Views on Hell,* Preston Sprinkle gives a vital warning we all should consider:

> If you hold onto your view too tightly, unwilling to reexamine it in light of Scripture, then you are placing your traditions and presuppositions on a higher pedestal than Scripture itself. If the view you have always believed is indeed Scriptural, then there's nothing to fear by considering and wrestling with other views. If Scripture is clear, then such clarity will be manifest. But there's a chance that the view you currently hold to is not a biblical one. And we all, therefore, need to be open to having our preconceived views corrected by Scripture.[1]

We need to be willing to reexamine and reconsider *any* belief we hold to make sure it actually is biblical.

There's a wonderful question in the Free Church tradition that has been used for this very purpose: *Where stands it written?* Where is this belief we hold actually taught in Scripture? Are we rightly understanding the pertinent Scriptures? This process of reexamining and reconsidering our beliefs about hell is what this book is about. In the next chapter, we'll look more closely at how we should approach this kind of process. But let me say now that I don't encourage anyone to change their views regarding these things too quickly. Take your time. Read this book prayerfully, with an open Bible, ready to check and verify what I've written. And then maybe read through some of the resources I've listed at the end of this book. It's not easy to accept a belief that most evangelical Christians still reject (and with which most aren't even truly familiar). But ultimately—especially as evangelical Christians—our commitment is above all else to biblical truth. The primary question for us is: *What does Scripture actually teach?*

I want to note the deep appreciation and respect I have for Thomas Talbott and Robin Parry. Their thinking on these issues has been challenging, compelling, and edifying. I also want to thank some of my friends who have especially provoked and encouraged my own thinking regarding these ideas over the years: Andy Eby, Peter Boehmer, Ric Rutherford, Jack Foster, and Doug Rosenfeld. I cannot thank enough my wonderful church family at The Orchard. They refuse to uncritically embrace or reject anything, but beautifully model a Berean approach of searching the Scriptures to see what is and isn't true (Acts 17:11). It's been encouraging to me to see the way my wife, Kelley, has thought through these issues for herself. I must express my heartfelt gratitude to my close friends who took the time to read this book and offer encouragement and input, with a special thank you to

---

1. Sprinkle, "Introduction," 14–15.

Mona Brackett for all her helpful feedback. And, of course, thanks to all of you for reading this book. I pray it will be a blessing to you. And now, when you're ready, let's turn to the next chapter . . . and spend some time thinking about hell.

Chapter Two

The Challenge of Hell

MOST EVANGELICAL CHRISTIANS BELIEVE hell is eternal. They accept as established truth the idea the lost (those who have not placed their faith in Jesus Christ) will suffer in hell forever. This is what we've been taught in church and from Scripture. We may struggle at times with thoughts of a never-ending hell, but that doesn't mean we don't believe it. We may completely trust what we've been taught about hell, and firmly believe this is what the Bible teaches. Yet when we think about people actually *experiencing* endless torment, with no possibility of relief—even though we may believe it—we wrestle with the reality of this belief.

Some Christians deal with this kind of unpleasantness by trying not to think about hell at all. If someone hasn't been deeply troubled by the concept of hell, they probably haven't spent much time contemplating it. But, sooner or later, most of us grapple with making some sense emotionally and theologically of hell. And we're not alone. John Stott once wrote of the idea of eternal suffering in hell:

> Emotionally, I find the concept intolerable and do not understand how people can live with it without either cauterizing their feelings or cracking under the strain.[1]

J. I. Packer expressed his own struggle with hell:

> Who can take pleasure in the thought of people being eternally lost? If you want to see folk damned, there is something wrong with you![2]

1. Stott, *Evangelical Essentials*, 314–15.
2. Packer, "Way of Salvation," 117.

C. S. Lewis wrote of hell:

> There is no doctrine which I would more willingly remove from
> Christianity than this, if it lay in my power.[3]

Few Christians relish the thought of unsaved people being subjected to
eternal conscious torment (or completely ceasing to exist), but we're committed to biblical truth and willing to faithfully believe what the Scriptures
teach us.

Some people, though, don't seem to have much trouble at all embracing the eternal suffering of the lost. For instance, read what Denny Burk
had to say about the never-ending torment of those in hell:

> This view of God's judgment is not a cause for embarrassment for
> Christians, but will ultimately become a source of joy and praise
> for the saints as they witness the infinite goodness and justice of
> God.[4]

Even many who believe in an eternal hell will recoil from this picture, but it
challenges us to reflect on our own response to hell. After all, hell is a part of
God's plan, something God himself incorporated into his ultimate solution
for the problem of sin and rebellion. How can we be embarrassed by God's
plan? Are *we* more loving and merciful than God? But yet . . . how could
we *not* struggle with the idea of eternal conscious suffering? So, we need to
be very clear about what the Scriptures actually teach, to either be firmly
convinced in our mind that this *is* the teaching of Scripture—or to see that
maybe this is *not* what the Bible teaches.

What Are the Different Views of Hell Evangelical Christians Hold?

Here's a brief description of each view:

Eternal Conscious Torment (or Punishment)

This is the default view for most of us, and it's certainly the belief most familiar to the vast majority of people reading this book. It's the well-known
teaching that those who have died without placing their faith in Christ will

3. Lewis, *Problem of Pain*, 119–20.
4. Burk, "Eternal Conscious Torment," 20.

go to hell, where they will suffer for eternity without hope of any release or end to their torment.

That any sincere, Bible-believing Christians have a view of hell *other* than this one may be a complete surprise to you! Of course, I can remember a time when I assumed all Christians believed as I did about the events leading up to the return of Christ, too. *Surely*—I thought at the time—*all Bible-believing Christians agree that before Christ returns there will be a rapture of the church followed by a seven-year tribulation.* Just because we're not familiar with the views of other believers, doesn't mean we can simply assume all true Christians believe the same as we do. We need to take the time to understand other views.

Annihilationism (or Conditionalism)

Most scholars and pastors know of this view, and this awareness has grown steadily since the 1980s. There's a significant minority of evangelical believers who share this understanding of hell, and prominent books and conferences advocating it. These Christians believe that when the Bible describes the wages of our sin as "death," it means death in the sense of actually ceasing to consciously exist. According to this view, those who have died without placing their faith in Christ will go to hell, where they will suffer for a certain amount of time but will be ultimately consumed, they will finally die, and will completely cease to exist.

Universal Reconciliation and Restoration

This view has been experiencing a resurgence among evangelical Christians the past two decades or so, and interest in it seems to be growing. Those who hold this view believe that God not only loves each person and desires that each person be saved, but that he will ultimately accomplish his desire by bringing each individual person to salvation through faith in Christ, completely triumphing over hell and death. It's the teaching that those who have died without placing their faith in Christ will experience the judgment of hell, but that hell is finally both loving and redemptive, that it accomplishes God's purpose of bringing even the most obstinate sinner to the point of repentance and faith in Jesus Christ, and thus God will completely restore his creation.

Two of these views may be completely new to you, and even sound very strange. Notice that each view includes the reality of hell and judgment. None of these views deny the existence of hell, so it would be inaccurate to describe this discussion as between those who "believe in hell" and those who do not. Christians who hold each of these positions take sin and its consequences very seriously. Each understanding also insists on faith in Jesus Christ as absolutely essential for salvation, and that there is salvation in no one else but Christ (Acts 4:12). None of these views contradict any core, essential teaching of historical, biblical Christianity, and proponents of each view build their case drawing directly from Scripture. Where they differ is in how they understand, in light of Scripture, the purpose and final outcome of hell.

In this book, we'll be reexamining the eternal conscious torment view, and we'll also spend time considering the universal reconciliation and restoration view. This view is also known as universal salvation, Christian universalism, evangelical universalism, biblical universalism, ultimate reconciliation, universal restoration, etc. I'll use most of these names at various points in the book. But it's important to note that this view is very different from the "universalism" you may have heard about in the past. What we'll be looking at is *not* the idea that "all roads lead to heaven," or that everyone will be saved regardless of what they believe or in whom they trust. The universalism we'll be examining is thoroughly Christian and even evangelical in nature, intentionally grounded in Scripture and faith in Christ. (Of course, when we examine this view, we'll see together just how sound this scriptural basis is or is not.)

Much of what we'll cover in this book will also apply to the annihilationism or conditionalism view, but you may have noticed I don't include an in-depth examination of this position. My purpose is not to equally explore all the different views, but to provide an accessible introduction to the universal restoration perspective, comparing it to the traditional eternal conscious torment view. There are books that compare all of these options, and I list some of these resources at the end of this book. I have also included an extra chapter that briefly looks at *What about Annihilationism?*

How Should We Approach This Kind of Study?

So, how do we begin exploring an issue such as this? I have a few suggestions:

First, we need to seek out any necessary background information. There are certain details we need to understand before trying to compare different views. So, in the next chapter, we'll go over the different words used in Scripture for hell, and what they meant in their original context. After that, we'll look at some of the history of how the earliest Christians understood hell.

For each view, we'll begin by delving into the *exegetical* case (that is, drawing from the explicit reading of Scripture). We'll carefully examine the foundational claims that pastors and teachers use to establish belief in eternal conscious torment. We'll also biblically explore the core question: *Will some people be eternally lost?* Those who hold both the eternal conscious torment view and the annihilationism view would say, "Yes, some people will be eternally lost." But those who believe in universal reconciliation and restoration would disagree, saying, "No, no one will be eternally lost. God will ultimately reconcile and restore all of his creation." We'll see which scriptural case is the strongest.

After studying the key biblical passages for a particular view, we'll look at the broader *theological* arguments people commonly use to support it, and any theological challenges (especially challenges to universal reconciliation). We'll also be considering some vital questions: How does the biblical character of God affect how we understand this issue? Which view is most in harmony with the scriptural teachings of the gospel of Jesus Christ? Which best fits into the whole span of the biblical story? How does each view deal with scriptural themes such as judgment, love, forgiveness, justice, mercy, death, reconciliation, punishment, restoration, and victory?

As a pastor and teacher, I've spent a great deal of time examining differing theological views. You've probably done the same thing. It's not hard to find someone with an impressive list of Scripture passages and persuasive arguments that make their position sound thoroughly convincing—especially if we're just hearing their side! But I'm looking for more than that. I want to hear someone who can take the *other side's* list of Scripture passages, and explain *their* preferred Scriptures better than *they* do. I'm looking for the view that makes the best sense of *all* of Scripture, not just a narrow list of proof texts and untested arguments.

When observing an exchange between a Calvinist and an Arminian, for example, I want to see if the Arminian can give a better understanding of the ninth chapter of Romans, if the Calvinist can give a better understanding of Rom 11, and which one makes the best sense of *all* of Rom

9–11. (If you have no idea what a Calvinist or an Arminian is, you can see the final chapter in this book for a bit more on these differing views.) I want to know whose interpretation best fits the flow of the whole letter to the Romans and the context of the rest of Scripture. So, in considering differing views of hell, I want to see who can best explain *all* of the relevant passages and who can present the most biblically and theologically comprehensive and coherent view.

This might surprise you, but none of these views are based primarily on appeals to our emotions. And this is important. We want to make sure we're not embracing any belief because of our emotional preferences. However, we also can't divorce our emotions from a study that includes concepts such as the love of God, restoration of relationships, and the suffering of judgment. If we tried to remove all the passages in Scripture that speak of emotions or those that intentionally affect our emotions, we'd be cutting out a huge chunk of the Bible!

It might be helpful to think of our emotions in a similar way as a warning light on the dashboard of our car. When a light suddenly comes on, this could indicate something's wrong with the car, or it could just mean a malfunctioning sensor. Either way, something needs to be addressed. If we're hearing some belief we've never heard before, and it causes a strong, visceral reaction in us, what does this mean? It could be telling us either there's something profoundly wrong with the idea, or there's something wrong with our perception of it. Either way, we need to do some digging to determine whether it's *our feelings* that are out of sync with Scripture or this new (to us) belief. So, we recognize this kind of issue will touch us emotionally, and we don't ignore our emotional responses. But we don't make our emotions the court of final appeal.

How does this work? Let me give you one example. I hesitate to use this particular illustration because I don't want to alienate any readers (*in the second chapter, no less!*). But I think it's helpful to show the approach I'm describing. So, if you happen to disagree with me regarding the issue I'm about to use as an example, please be patient with me, hear my heart, and see past the issue itself to the point I'm trying to make.

Before I was able to serve vocationally in pastoral ministry, I worked for a few years in business management. I worked *with* female peers and worked *for* female supervisors. I've seen wonderful managers—men and women, and I've seen horrible managers—men and women. The effectiveness of any manager never had anything to do with their gender. So, I was inclined from the beginning to embrace a more egalitarian view of gender roles in church ministry, with no distinction at all in church leadership roles for men and women. Especially considering my views on church leadership—that each church should be led by a team of coequal pastoral elders without a designated senior or lead pastor—it would have been so easy to simply include women in our team of church pastors (or elders).

And so I've tried to read all the major books and articles from the different views on this issue, being perfectly willing to be convinced of the egalitarian view. But I'm not just looking for a view that's plausible, one that's convincing *enough*. For me as a pastor, it not only has to be a view I can accept, it has to be a view I can *teach* consistently and faithfully from Scripture. And if it's a view I'd *like* to believe, I'm even more careful to make sure I'm not simply seeing what I want to see. Don't forget, I teach the people in our church interactively—and they're not shy about asking probing questions! So, any view I hold has to stand up to the scrutiny of that kind of interactive study! The more I sought out books and articles presenting the egalitarian view, the more convinced I became of the soundness of the complementarian view—that men and women are equal but with different roles in church leadership. Culturally, I'm a reluctant complementarian, but scripturally, I'm convinced this is the design of God. (*Why* God would design it this way, and how we live out these biblical principles, are questions for an entirely different book!)

Now, some will strongly agree with me, and others will just as strongly disagree. But the issue itself is not my point (and I'm always willing to reconsider my viewpoint). I'm also not holding myself up as some perfect standard of balance, implying that you can therefore trust *my* conclusions. I'm only saying this is the way I try to process different claims of biblical truth, even to the point of rejecting views I'd like to embrace. And this is the kind of approach I think we all need to take in examining these kinds of issues.

If you're reading this, I assume you accept the Bible as our authoritative standard for what we believe and do as Christians. This is well and good. But we need to make sure we don't slip into viewing our own *interpretations* of Scripture as the standard for all Christians. And this is very easy to do. I believe the Bible is inerrant, completely free from error in everything it affirms as true. But my interpretations of Scripture are most definitely *not* inerrant!

If we're not willing to consider an alternative viewpoint regarding a belief such as hell, then we're dangerously close to assuming our own omniscience, that we already have all knowledge and perfectly understand all truth. Of course, that would make us God and we know that's not true! There's a logical fallacy known as "invincible ignorance." This is the attitude that *"I've already made up my mind, and no one can convince me I'm wrong!"* It's the adult version of plugging our ears and saying, *"I can't hear you, I can't hear you, I can't hear you."* This is *not* an appropriate attitude for followers of Christ.

We like to say that we "just go by the Bible," but we always study the Bible from the perspective of our traditions, our preconceptions, and often, our lack of knowledge regarding the original context of what was written. *Nobody* just goes by the Bible (at least not without a lot of ongoing work), and it's actually kind of arrogant for us to think that—in two thousand years of church history—*we're* somehow the ones who automatically have the untainted, unobstructed view of what the Bible is actually saying. This doesn't mean we can't come to real, confident conclusions, but we need to make sure we've done our homework. This also means we've taken the time to truly understand alternative viewpoints before we disagree with them or dismiss them.

Ultimately, we may not be convinced of a new view (new to us, that is); that's fine. But we need to be humble enough to acknowledge that we *could* be wrong. And we need to be willing to change our views if that's where a careful study of God's Word leads us. I love the old saying:

> If you never have to change your mind,
> you're probably not using it.

So, we're willing to change our minds—when necessary—but we're first going to rigorously, *scripturally* examine both the traditional view of hell and belief in universal salvation. We're going to push up our sleeves and do our homework. Amen?

Chapter Three

Hell in the Bible

Understanding the Biblical Words

WE OFTEN HEAR OF someone being "baptized," or refer to a person as a "deacon" in the church. We use these words all the time in church life. But we may not know that these familiar English words, and many others, actually come to us directly from the original Greek. For instance, when it's time to "baptize" someone, we take our name for this practice from the Greek word *baptizo*. When we speak of a "deacon" in the church, this comes from the Greek word *diakonos*. "Apostle" comes from *apostolos*, and "angel" comes from *angelos*. It's fun to know how many of the words we commonly use in the church today have simply been adapted from the very same Greek words the early church used in the first century.

While this is true of many words we use, it's not the case when we talk about hell. There are three different words in the original languages that have often been translated as "hell." But what *we* mean when we speak of hell is very different from what these Hebrew and Greek words meant. Before we start digging into Scripture, it's helpful for us to know what these words are, and what each means (especially in their original context). It makes sense for us to start with the Old Testament, which means we need to discuss:

Sheol

In early English translations of the Bible such as the King James Version, the Hebrew word *Sheol* was often translated as "hell." (In some later versions, they didn't even translate it, but just left it as "Sheol.") In most current translations, you won't find the word "hell" at all in the Old Testament. Instead Sheol is usually translated as "the grave," but it can also descriptively refer to "the pit" or "the depths." Sheol was a somewhat vague concept. It referred to the state of being physically dead (hence "the grave"), but scholars debate whether the ancient Jews understood this to be a location or even a conscious state.[1] However it was experienced, Sheol was the destiny of everyone after they died; the righteous and the unrighteous alike—it didn't matter—everyone went to the grave in the Old Testament.

This is all very interesting, but the Hebrew concept of Sheol doesn't tell us anything about the fate of those who fail to place their faith in Christ before they die. The Old Testament passages that use this word aren't telling us anything about *hell*. So, now we move on to the New Testament.

Hades

There was a span of four hundred years between the end of the Old Testament and the birth of Christ (what we refer to as the "intertestamental period"). During this time, Jewish understanding of the grave developed in ways that went beyond the explicit references found in the Old Testament Scriptures. Some claim these changes were due to influences on early Jewish culture that came from Egyptian, Persian, and Greek ideas of the afterlife.

Regardless, because Greek increasingly became the common language throughout the Mediterranean region (even for Jewish people), it became ordinary practice for Jews to use the Greek word *Hades* in place of the Hebrew "Sheol." Hades had much the same meaning as Sheol, it was the grave or the "place of the dead." And, as with Sheol, Hades was the fate of everyone who died, righteous or unrighteous. Many Jewish people would now often include the idea (possibly drawing from outside influences such as Greek mythology) of some kind of separation within Hades (for example, see Luke 16:19–31, which we'll discuss in a later chapter).

"Hades" is used ten times in the New Testament: Matt 11:23; 16:18; Luke 10:15; 16:23; Acts 2:27, 31; Rev 1:18; 6:8; 20:13, 14. Notice that neither of these words, Sheol nor Hades, refers to what happens to the lost after judgment or to where someone might spend eternity. So, these words in Scripture (and these passages) don't tell us anything about the eternal

---

1. Harris et al., *Theological Wordbook*, 892.

fate of the unsaved. These words refer only to the grave—the state of being dead—not to what we think of in Christian theology as hell.

Gehenna

You may have heard that "Jesus mentioned hell more than anyone else in the Bible." Of course, as we just saw, Hades is more accurately translated "the grave" or "the place of the dead" rather than hell. So, none of the ten verses that use this word should be considered as references to *hell*. Another word Jesus used that's often been translated as "hell" is *Gehenna*. What do we know about Gehenna?

The first thing we should be aware of is that Gehenna was, and still is, a literal place. It's a valley just southwest of the old city of Jerusalem. The Greek word "Gehenna" comes from the Hebrew *ge Hinnom*. We see this place referenced in the Old Testament as the "Valley of Hinnom" or sometimes the "Valley of the Sons of Hinnom."

So, what significance do we see in the Old Testament and in history for the Valley of Hinnom or Gehenna? There were four events specifically associated with Gehenna:

1. Gehenna was the valley outside Jerusalem where some of the people of Israel sacrificed their children, burning them on altars to the pagan god Molech. (See 2 Chr 28:1–3; 33:6.)

2. These idolatrous altars in Gehenna were later defiled and broken up, and the valley was cleansed of these horrific child sacrifices. (See 2 Kgs 23:10–16.)

3. God spoke through the Old Testament prophet Jeremiah of a coming judgment on his people that would be carried out in the Valley of Hinnom (Gehenna). (See Jer 7; 19; 32:32–35.)

4. In AD 70, the Roman general Titus—responding to the Jewish rebellion—slaughtered the inhabitants of Jerusalem, and destroyed the city. The bodies of the dead were thrown into Gehenna, and later disposed of by burning.

Today, when we read in Scripture warnings of Israel being burned in fire, we immediately think of hell. But the ancient Jewish people, hearing this from the perspective of the Old Testament Scriptures, would have associated this fire with the *judgment* of God. Prior to the ministry of Jesus, though, the word "Gehenna" began taking on different connotations with some Jewish teachers. They seemed to merge the fire associated with judgment in the literal Gehenna (or Valley of Hinnom) into their developing concept of Hades, with the righteous going to Paradise and the unrighteous to "Gehenna," used now in a metaphorical sense for a fiery place of torment after death. There was widespread disagreement among these Jewish teachers concerning the nature and duration of this "Gehenna." In fact, it seems they debated just about *everything* having to do with this new concept of Gehenna (who would go there, how long they would be there, what would be the final outcome, etc.).[2]

As I mentioned earlier, some observe that Jesus talked about hell more than anyone else in the Bible. But, as we've seen, the places where he speaks of Hades would be referring to the grave, not hell. It is very true, though, that Jesus used the word "Gehenna" more than anyone else in Scripture. The word is found twelve times in the New Testament (Matt 5:22, 29, 30; 10:28; 18:9; 23:15, 33; Mark 9:43, 45, 47; Luke 12:5; Jas 3:6), and all but one of these are in the words of Christ in the Gospels (and these only in the synoptic Gospels: Matthew, Mark, and Luke). So, what did *Jesus* mean by Gehenna? Biblical scholars have different views. (I should note that many of these references are of parallel accounts in the Gospels, and we actually only know of four separate occasions when Jesus spoke of Gehenna.)

Some think when Jesus used the word "Gehenna" he meant hell, or, more accurately, a place of torment within Hades intended for the wicked, much as some other Jewish teachers in his day taught. Others aren't so convinced. In the Old Testament "ge Hinnom" never refers to anything like hell. It's always speaking of the literal Valley of Hinnom. Was Jesus following these contemporary Jewish teachers in their new understanding of Gehenna, or was he using Gehenna in a way that would be consistent with Jeremiah and every other Old Testament reference?

This question is especially meaningful when we consider how Jesus was always challenging their shared assumptions and understandings regarding what were, to them, familiar concepts such as Messiah, kingdom, etc. When Jesus talked about the Messiah and the kingdom of God, he had to dispel their common misunderstandings of these ideas. Wouldn't it make sense that he was doing the same thing when he talked about Gehenna? Many scholars conclude that when Jesus spoke of Gehenna, he was doing so in a way consistent with the Old Testament pattern of references,

2. Jersak, *Never Be Shut*, 33–67.

following the understanding of Jeremiah, and applying this to the coming judgment of Israel, particularly Jerusalem, in AD 70.

There's another aspect of this we need to consider. If Gehenna was such a common word for "hell" among most first-century Jewish people, it's curious that—other than one passing reference by James—Jesus is the only one in the New Testament who used this word. Why is that? Paul never used this word; Peter never used this word; John never used this word (even in his Gospel); the author of Hebrews didn't use this word. This word was only used by Jesus when ministering in a distinctly Jewish setting, and otherwise only once by James in a very early letter, *also* in a predominantly Jewish context. (You can check out Jas 1:1 to see this Jewish context.)

Paul often used other distinctly Jewish words and concepts in his letters—but not this one. John used the word "Hades" four times in Revelation, but—in this book that so emphasized final judgment, and where Old Testament language and imagery are woven continually and thoroughly all through the text—he never used the word "Gehenna." If this word, with strong connotations of judgment in the Old Testament, actually did convey the fiery torment of all the lost, it would be quite surprising that John didn't use it even once in Revelation.

So, there's a noticeable, stark contrast between the way Jesus used this word and the complete absence of the word in the writings of the apostles (after the extremely early, distinctly Jewish-oriented, sole reference of James). When we see this, it's hard to ignore the likely conclusion that Jesus is referring to the judgment of Jerusalem to come, which would be so vividly, literally, and historically fulfilled in the actual Gehenna. This would follow the strong pattern of both John the Baptist and Jesus warning of this very judgment: Matt 3:7–10; 23:37–38; 24:1–2; Mark 13:1–2; Luke 3:7–9; 19:41–44; 21:5–6, 20–24.

So, when we begin to look at what Scripture tells us about hell, we need to first recognize that the Old Testament doesn't say anything explicitly about hell per se. (It does have a lot to say about judgment, of course, and we'll look at this later in the book.) Many of the New Testament passages we may have thought speak of hell, such as the references to Hades, are actually speaking of death or the grave, not hell. And even the Gehenna passages are likely referring, not to hell or Hades, but to the judgment of Israel in AD 70.

What does all this mean for us? It only means that when we're trying to determine what Scripture is teaching about hell, we shouldn't rely on

Bible verses that speak of Sheol, Hades, or Gehenna. This still leaves a great many passages that are inarguably speaking of hell, and so are relevant to our study. For instance, the "lake of fire" is referenced in Revelation, and Jesus spoke of both "eternal fire" and "eternal punishment."

For our purposes, we need to focus on the most clear passages, and so we'll look at these verses in context very soon. But first, as we turn to examining the traditional eternal conscious torment view, we need to understand how the early Christians understood hell. Did they all believe what most evangelical Christians today do about hell? Let's find out.

PART TWO

Why Should We Believe Hell Is Eternal?

Examining the Case for Eternal Conscious Torment

Chapter Four

Hell in the Early Church
What Did They Believe?

As an evangelical pastor, there have been times I've had to explain, or even defend, hell. More precisely, I was explaining and defending *eternal conscious torment* in hell. I didn't do this because I loved the idea of endless punishment, or because I'm a "hellfire-and-brimstone preacher." I understood this view to be the clear biblical teaching. Explaining and defending hell this way was something I felt I *had* to do in order to be a biblically faithful pastor.

On these occasions, I always fell back on what I saw as the two solid foundations for belief in an endless hell:

1. the unequivocal wording of Scripture.

2. the consistent view of the church throughout history.

I can look back now at email exchanges between me and people who were questioning hell and see where I consistently relied on these two claims. And I wasn't alone in this; it's easy to find Christian pastors and teachers basing their support of eternal conscious torment on these two core ideas.

When we study Scripture, we know we shouldn't interpret the Bible in a vacuum. By that I mean we can't just rely on our own unique, personal interpretations of what the Bible means without thought of anyone else. We should study the Scriptures privately, of course. But even then, we're very aware of studying as part of a larger community of Christians who are all reading and studying the same Bible. This is part of the reason why we consult study Bibles, and why we study together in small group Bible studies and in our church congregations. The Scripture tells us "iron sharpens iron" (Prov 27:17), and this is true in our study of the Scriptures.

As a pastor and teacher, it's my responsibility to be aware of how other pastors and teachers understand the passages I'm teaching. Part of the process of biblical interpretation is to compare my work to those of others. I read commentaries to see what biblical scholars tell us about the Scriptures I'm studying. I seek to be knowledgeable about how others in my church denomination or tradition understand the passage in question, and I need to know about views outside my own camp. How do those of other Christian traditions understand these same Scriptures?

But this process doesn't end here. I also need to ask: What about Christians in other parts of the world, in different cultural contexts? And it's important to know how Christian scholars and pastors have understood these biblical passages throughout the history of the church. To say that a particular belief has always been the view of the church would be a powerful statement and could seem strongly convincing, but it's one we need to verify.

Most evangelical Christians aren't that familiar with early church writers and teachers, and that's unfortunate for many reasons. Because of our lack of historical awareness, we tend to assume the early Christians worshiped pretty much the same way we do every Sunday, and that they believed exactly the same things we do. When we're thinking of hell, for instance, even many pastors assume that the vast majority of early church pastors and leaders believed in eternal conscious torment as do the majority of evangelicals today. But is this true?

If pressed, some pastors may have some vague recollection that the early Christian scholar Origen held to some form of universalism. And we might even be aware that annihilationists or conditionalists claim Irenaeus as an early proponent of their view. But we would usually consider these people to be outliers in the early history of the church, brilliant theologians who may have been a bit eccentric in some of their beliefs, but overall were exceptions that prove the rule in an otherwise consistently held—and familiar—view of hell. But is this actually the case? It might be good to make sure the early consensus to which we refer did, in fact, exist.

The desire by many to go back and see what these early Christians actually wrote about their beliefs regarding hell has proved a challenge to this common assumption. It's not that this kind of research had never been done before, but there is definitely a renewed—and growing—interest in understanding with greater clarity *who* believed *what* about final judgment. The results are both fascinating and surprising. (If history really isn't your thing, stick with me for the next few pages! I'll make this as painless as possible, and I'll bring it all together at the end to explain why this is so important.)

A few years ago, for a study on church history, I put together a list of key leaders in the first five hundred years of the church. This class had nothing to do with views on hell, and such a question wasn't even part of my thinking when I compiled this list. The only thing I did to distinguish these early church leaders was to separately list the Greek-speaking and writing church thinkers from those who spoke and wrote in Latin. This wasn't an exhaustive list of early Christian leaders (it was a one-page handout, after all), but it included those I considered most significant for a leadership class on church history.

When I began reexamining my claim that eternal conscious torment has been the consistent view of the historical church, I remembered this list. So—just for fun—I used this preexisting list as a test to see how predominant my traditional view actually was in the early church. There were twenty-three names on the list. The first thing I did was to note—based on what I was reading from church historians—which of the early leaders on this list clearly advocated eternal conscious torment.

From this list of twenty-three prominent Christians thinkers in the first five hundred years of the history of the church, five explicitly taught this understanding of hell:

Tertullian

Cyprian of Carthage

John Chrysostom

Jerome

Augustine

Now, please understand, I'm not saying these are the *only* leaders in the early church who believed in eternal conscious torment! But they were the only ones listed *on this particular handout* who we know held this view.

Next, I noted those who taught an annihilationist or conditionalist view of hell. On this list, there was only one proponent of annihilationism, but it was a very significant name:

Irenaeus of Lyons

Again, this doesn't mean he was the only one in the early church who held this view, just that he was the only one on my list! And Irenaeus was no lightweight; many consider him the first systematic theologian of the church.

I should also note that the first five names on the list were inconclusive regarding this question:

Clement of Rome

Ignatius of Antioch

Polycarp of Smyrna

Papias of Hierapolis

Justin Martyr

Of course, we should remember from the last chapter that the Jews of the first century didn't have one consistent understanding of "hell," but held very differing views. So, it's actually not surprising that we just don't know what these earliest church leaders believed regarding hell.

Okay, so what about universal reconciliation and restoration? How many early church thinkers taught a Christian universalist view? I first noted the Christian leaders from this period for whom we could be certain—from their clear writings—that they held this view:

Clement of Alexandria

Origen

Dionysius of Alexandria

Pamphilus of Caesarea

Eusebius of Caesarea

Athanasius

Gregory of Nyssa

Jerome

Augustine

The observant reader may now be protesting that I *already* listed Jerome and Augustine as believing in eternal conscious torment! These two leaders are listed twice because they first believed in universal salvation, but then later came to embrace eternal conscious torment. (There were other significant changes in their theology, as well.)

Anyway, you can understand how shocked I was! I had been high-lighting in different colors to represent the different views, and the results were jaw-dropping. Not only was eternal conscious torment not the historical consensus of the church, it would be hard to argue it was even the predominant view! This effect was even more striking when I noted on my list those who we couldn't prove conclusively were Christian universalists, but who almost certainly were:

Hilary of Poitiers

Basil of Caesarea

Gregory Nazianzen

Ambrose of Milan

Cyril of Alexandria

Clearly the consensus of at least the Christians in the first five hundred years of the church was quite different than what I had understood.

Ilaria Ramelli is a respected scholar of historical theology (among other things). In 2013, she published the results of sixteen years of pains-taking research of early Christian views concerning universal salvation and restoration (*apokatastasis* in the Greek).[1] Ramelli's work was widely hailed for its impressive span and depth. Reviewers also noted the great care she took in evaluating these ancient authors' statements in the context of their larger bodies of work, in light of Scripture, and in their historical contexts. Many of her fellow scholars now view her book as a new benchmark on the subject of universal salvation in the early church. One scholar, Michael McClymond, attempted an extensive critique of her work.[2] In a more recent book, Ramelli quite capably responded to McClymond's challenges, show-ing his conclusions to be unsupported by the actual historical data.[3]

Ramelli corrected the overreach of some earlier universalists who had tried to show this belief to have been the standard view in the early church. But she also surprised almost everyone by exhaustively documenting just *how* extensive belief in universal salvation actually was. Christian univer-salism was not merely the extreme minority view of one or two isolated

1. Ramelli, *Apokatastasis*.

2. McClymond, *Devil's Redemption*.

3. Ramelli, *Larger Hope*, 222–62.

thinkers; it was widely held, and taught by many of the people we consider to be great heroes of the early Christian faith.

Origen was by no means the first Christian universalist. We know that before him there were at least Bardaisan of Edessa and Clement of Alexandria. (There are also indications of belief in universal salvation in Christian writings preceding these teachers. We just don't know the view of many early church leaders because they either didn't address the issue or didn't make clear enough their view.) We shouldn't move too quickly past Origen himself, though. Possessing an imposing intellect, he's the only Christian thinker in the first centuries of the church who produced more writing on theology and biblical exposition than did Augustine.

It would take far too long to go through all of the early Christian leaders who believed in universal salvation, but we should comment on a few highly significant examples. Some may be aware (as I listed earlier) that Gregory of Nyssa firmly held a belief in universal salvation and restoration. This is clear in his writings and has been well-documented by historical theologians. Again, this is worth noting because Gregory of Nyssa was one of the most respected theologians of the fourth century, one of the famous "Cappadocian fathers." (The early church leaders are often referred to as the "church fathers.") Gregory of Nyssa was even honored by the Second Council of Nicea as "father of fathers." Gregory's views on universal salvation were well-known, running through virtually all of his writings, and apparently did nothing to hamper the respect or acclaim he garnered from his fellow church scholars and leaders.

Ramelli showed that, while not as clear or outspoken as Gregory of Nyssa, we should include the other Cappadocians, Basil of Caesarea and Gregory Nazianzen, as revered theologians in the early church who evidenced belief in universal reconciliation and restoration.[4] We see good reason to include the great champion of the Trinity, Athanasius, among the universalists![5] Even Augustine believed in universal salvation until later in life, as was also true of Jerome, and both commented on how prevalent the belief still was at that time. Jerome even claimed that *most* Christians of his day believed in universal reconciliation and restoration.[6] This is just a sampling of a much longer list of prominent Christian theologians in the

---

4. Ramelli, *Larger Hope*, 100–109, 130–34.
5. Ramelli, *Larger Hope*, 86–92.
6. Ramelli, *Larger Hope*, 148–50, 154–58.

first five hundred years of the history of the church whose theological work incorporated belief in universal salvation.

If we want to understand what the early Christians thought about certain issues, a good place to look is in the early creeds. The creeds were summary statements of what Christians believed. They were formally adopted by official church councils made up of the gathered leaders of all the churches. But when we turn to the early church creeds to see what all Christians believed about hell, any such belief is noticeably absent. It's telling that none of the early creeds include anything at all concerning eternal damnation in hell! And the fact that Christian leaders and theologians held differing views regarding hell didn't seem to them a great cause for concern or debate—at least until Augustine. Even Augustine didn't condemn those who disagreed with the view of hell he had come to adopt in his later life (eternal conscious torment).

We should also notice how many of the early church leaders and thinkers who spoke and wrote in Greek believed in and taught universalism. And we take note that those who advocated for eternal conscious torment tended almost exclusively to be those who spoke and wrote in Latin. Why is this important? Because the New Testament was written in Greek. And those who thought, spoke, read, and wrote in Greek would naturally have much greater understanding and insight into the meaning of these Greek writings. The meaning of certain words in the Greek Scriptures became one of the distinguishing points between the views, and the understanding of the early Greek-speaking scholars would have carried much more weight than those who weren't as conversant in Greek. We'll look at this in much greater depth in the next chapter.

We've only skimmed the surface of these different views of hell represented in the first five hundred years of the history of the church. While, over time, universal salvation became a distinctly minority view (particularly in the Western church), there continued to be Christian leaders and pastors who held this view throughout the history of the church. We don't have time to explore later Christian universalists such as the seventeenth-century Puritan universalist Peter Sterry, men who were associated with George Whitefield who came to embrace universalism such as James Relly and John Murray, eighteenth-century Baptist universalist Elhanan Winchester, or universalist authors such as Hannah Whitall Smith and George MacDonald.[7] (Since I'm writing as an evangelical pastor, I won't even

7. Parry, *Larger Hope*.

attempt addressing the vast number of Eastern Orthodox believers and clergy who have believed in Christian universalism, or the many Roman Catholic theologians who have embraced a hopeful universalism.)

So, what do we learn from all of this? Does this tell us which view is right and which ones are wrong? No, it doesn't. We still have a lot of examining to do before we can reach these kinds of conclusions. But looking at this background does keep us from falsely claiming any one view as *the* overwhelmingly dominant view in the early church. Some overeager proponents of universalism have tried to make it the virtually universal view of early Christians. There's simply not enough evidence to back up this claim. But we have even *less* evidence to suggest that eternal conscious torment was the predominant view in the early church.

However we may debate the specific view of any particular scholar of the early church (and these debates will continue), it seems incontrovertible that the early church of the first five centuries included varying understandings of hell and final judgment. Remember, we began the chapter with the two foundational claims on which many of us have based a solid belief in eternal conscious torment:

1. the unequivocal wording of Scripture.

2. the consistent view of the church throughout history.

We've now examined some of the early church views regarding hell. *Has eternal conscious torment been the consistent view of the church throughout history?* No, it has not. It definitely wasn't the consensus view, or even the majority view, for the first five hundred years of the life of the church.

This means the second foundational claim above fails to stand under examination, and it's *not* a basis for belief in eternal conscious torment. We simply can't assume one view as *the* Christian view historically. And this makes our continuing study even more necessary if we want to understand what the Bible actually teaches us about hell. And so, after looking at the necessary background data and context, we're now ready to turn to the Scriptures.

Chapter Five

What about the "Eternal Fire" of Hell?

As I shared in the last chapter, there have been times when I've had to explain and defend belief in eternal conscious torment. When this was necessary, I always relied on the same two foundational claims:

1. the unequivocal wording of Scripture.
2. the consistent view of the church throughout history.

As we saw in the last chapter, it's not really appropriate to speak of a consensus regarding the nature of hell in the early life of the church. This means the second claim above is not true. There *was no* consistent view of hell in the first five hundred years of church history. And while we shouldn't argue that universal restoration was the dominant view in the church during this time, it's certain from the historical evidence that eternal conscious torment was definitely *not* the consensus of the early church.

We also saw that the Greek-speaking and writing leaders and teachers in the early church tended more toward a biblical universalism, while the Latin-speaking leaders and teachers gravitated to the eternal conscious torment view. This is significant because the New Testament was written in Greek—and that obviously includes all the relevant hell passages. This leaves a nagging question we have to address:

> If the wording in these *Greek* Scriptures requiring an eternal hell is as clear and unequivocal as we think it is, why did so many *Greek*-speaking teachers in the early church believe that ultimately everyone would be saved and restored?

When we read our English translations, the wording of Scripture certainly *seems* to be unequivocal and inescapable. When addressing this issue in the past, I always turned to the three passages I felt speak most clearly about the nature of hell. I would begin with Matt 25:41–46, which uses the phrases "eternal fire" and "eternal punishment" (contrasting this with "eternal life"):

> Then he will also say to those on his left, "Depart from me, you who are cursed, into the eternal fire prepared for the devil and his angels! . . ." Then they will go away to eternal punishment, but the righteous to eternal life.

I would go from this passage to 2 Thess 1:8–9:

> He will punish those who do not know God and do not obey the gospel of our Lord Jesus. They will be punished with everlasting destruction and shut out from the presence of the Lord and from the glory of his might.

And finally I would turn to the vivid description in Rev 14:9–11:

> A third angel followed them and said in a loud voice: "If anyone worships the beast and its image and receives its mark on their forehead or on their hand, they, too, will drink the wine of God's fury, which has been poured full strength into the cup of his wrath. They will be tormented with burning sulfur in the presence of the holy angels and of the Lamb. And the smoke of their torment will rise for ever and ever. There will be no rest day or night for those who worship the beast and its image, or for anyone who receives the mark of its name."

It was hard to see how these passages could be any more clear. It seemed very evident from Scripture that the suffering in hell was, indeed, eternal.

So, when I first began hearing about an evangelical Christian form of universalism, I was curious how they would deal with these verses. When I heard the suggestion that the words "eternal" or "forever" in these passages don't *actually mean* eternal or forever, they mean "of the age to come," I was immediately suspicious. This can be a clever way of skirting around the obvious meaning of a text: "Oh, what this *really* means is . . ." My initial thought was that the people who believed this other view weren't able to deal with these passages, so they were grasping at straws to explain them away.

But I also had a nagging awareness that didn't let me dismiss this claim so easily. I knew that tradition *does* sometimes influence the choices of scholars in translating the Bible. For instance, in Eph 4:11 there's no reason why the word *poimenas* (the plural form of *poimen*) is translated "pastors" except for tradition. Variations of this word are found eighteen times in the New Testament; seventeen of those times the word is translated "shepherd(s)." It's only this one verse where the word "pastors" is used. The word *ekklesia* wasn't a religious word at all in the first century, but a common one connoting an assembly or association of people, yet it's usually translated "church." Again, this is due to tradition. There are many other examples we could list. So, it wouldn't be unprecedented for tradition to influence the translation of certain words in these hell passages. And I had to acknowledge we were loading a great deal of belief regarding hell on the back of one solitary Greek word.

At some point, I began to run across (without looking for them) surprising comments from solidly conservative, evangelical scholars concerning this word. I kept finding trusted authors acknowledging that the Greek word for "eternal" or "forever" in these passages doesn't actually mean eternal or forever. I want to stress both that I wasn't looking for these comments, and that these comments were coming from people whom I considered eminently trustworthy. Shockingly, they actually seemed to be saying much the same thing the Christian universalists were saying!

For instance, no less an authority than Greg Beale, in his monumental commentary on the book of Revelation, had this to say (commenting on Rev 20:10, but referring back to 14:11):

> Strictly speaking, even the expression "they will be tormented *forever and ever*" is figurative: *eis tous aionas ton aionon* literally can be rendered "unto the ages of the ages"; at the least, the phrase figuratively connotes a very long time. The context here and in the whole Apocalypse must determine whether this is a limited time or an unending period, and both indicate clearly that the expression refers to an unending period.[1]

To be clear, Beale sees eternal conscious torment in these passages, but he bases this on the *context* of the passages—not the unequivocal *meaning* of the words. We'll consider his contextual reasons for drawing this conclusion, and what "ages of ages" means, later in this chapter. But what I want us to notice now is how forthrightly Beale clarifies that this phrase does

---

1. Beale, *Revelation*, 1030; emphasis in original.

not literally mean "forever and ever," but "unto the ages of ages." He readily acknowledges this throughout his commentary on Revelation. If this is right, then we can't base belief in eternal conscious torment on the *meaning* of the word *aionios* (in its various Greek forms).

I noticed in the works of respected New Testament scholar F. F. Bruce that he consistently understood the word aionios in Scripture—usually translated "eternal"—to mean, *not* eternal, but "of the age (*aion*) to come."[2] Our church was, at that time, part of a theologically conservative, evangelical denomination, the Evangelical Free Church of America. The EFCA leaders had not only written a thoughtfully worded Statement of Faith, but they published a book, titled *Evangelical Convictions*, that helpfully served as the official theological exposition of our Statement of Faith. In this book, commenting on Matt 25:41, 46, our denominational leaders wrote, "It is true that the word translated 'eternal' here (aionios) means 'pertaining to the age to come'"![3] I should also note that some of these references went back decades, while others were quite recent.

As I mentioned before, some would argue that the word in question should somehow be understood as eternal in these contexts anyway (even though that's not what it means), and we'll consider these arguments a bit later in this chapter. But you can understand why I was so surprised to find theologically conservative stalwarts treating this seemingly unequivocal wording as . . . well . . . equivocal. They were actually saying the *same thing* the universalists were saying about this word—that it doesn't mean "eternal," but "of the age to come." And these weren't isolated exceptions. I found it hard to find *any* reputable scholar arguing that the word in these passages unambiguously means "eternal." Clearly, I needed to know more about the meaning of this Greek word.

There *is* a Greek word used in the New Testament (and in first-century literature) that consistently means "eternal." That word is *aidios*. This word isn't used in any of the hell passages we've quoted or anywhere the Scriptures are referring to the judgment of humanity. The word in question for us is aionios (and grammatical variations). The core of this word is the word *aion*, which is where we get our word *eon*.

Now, you always want to be careful whenever someone says: *"This is where we get our word . . ."* We can innocently take a *current* meaning for a word and plug it back into the *first century*. This often doesn't work and can

2. Bruce, *Gospel of John*, 89; "Age," 67.

3. Free Church, *Evangelical Convictions*, 250; Strand, "Eternal Conscious Punishment."

lead to a misunderstanding of Scripture. For instance, when Paul says in Rom 1:16 that the gospel is the *dynamis* of God, he wasn't saying the gospel is the "dynamite" of God! The Greek word *dynamis* may mean dynamite now, but it most certainly did not in the first century! We want to be careful to not make this kind of mistake.[4]

But the Greek word aion meant essentially the same thing in the first century it means today, so this word is typically translated "age" in the Bible. Here are some familiar passages that use the word aion:

> Grace and peace to you from God our Father and the Lord Jesus Christ, who gave himself for our sins to rescue us from the present evil age. (Gal 1:3–4)

> . . . when he raised Christ from the dead and seated him at his right hand in the heavenly realms, far above all rule and authority, power and dominion, and every name that is invoked, not only in the present age but also in the one to come. (Eph 1:20–21)

> . . . in order that in the coming ages he might show the incomparable riches of his grace, expressed in his kindness to us in Christ Jesus. (Eph 2:7)

We see in these passages that this word aion doesn't mean eternity, but "age." We even notice, in the first chapter of Ephesians, one age contrasted with another: "not only in the present age but also in the one to come." (Some translations use the word "world," as in: "not only in this world, but also in the world to come.")

Hopefully you can handle just a little grammar without your eyes glazing over! I hope so, because this is important, and I want to make sure we all understand it. Imagine the noun *congress*. Now, what would the *adjective* form of this word be? It would be congress*ional*, right? And what does the word *congressional* mean? It would mean "*pertaining to congress.*" Does this make sense so far?

Now, the word aion, that we've been looking at, is the *noun*. And the *adjective* form of aion is aionios. If the noun aion means "age," what would the adjective aionios mean? It would mean "*pertaining to the age,*" right? And this is exactly what we hear from trusted evangelical scholars, as I showed earlier in the chapter.

4. Carson, *Exegetical Fallacies*, 33–34.

Most evangelical scholars acknowledge that this word aionios doesn't mean eternal, but means "pertaining to the age." But many times they'll hedge this by saying the word doesn't . . . *necessarily* . . . mean eternal, or it . . . *may* . . . be translated differently. As part of her exhaustive study of early Christian leaders, and their beliefs concerning universal salvation, Ilaria Ramelli needed to determine precisely what this word meant to the people at that time. So, she and David Konstan completed the most extensive and detailed study of this word to date. They published this research in a separate book. Here's their conclusion:

> *Aionios* does *not* mean "eternal" . . . it has a wide range of meanings and its possible renderings are multiple, but it does not mean "eternal." In particular, when it is associated with life or punishment, in the Bible and in Christian authors who keep themselves close to the Biblical usage, it denotes their belonging to the world to come.[5]

I'm not aware of any challenge to this incredibly comprehensive research.

Ramelli and Konstan do write (in the same paragraph I just quoted) that the word aionios "acquires this meaning only when it refers to God, and only because the notion of eternity was included in the conception of God." What exactly does this mean?

Think of a Christian teacher using words such as "lasting" or "enduring" to refer to what's eternal. If I were to say to a group of people, "Do you want to invest your life in what is *temporary* or what is *lasting*?" does the word "lasting" mean eternal? No, it doesn't. But I would be using it to *refer* to what's eternal. So, in a sense, we could say "lasting" can mean "eternal" *in this sentence*—but only because what I'm referring to (eternal life) is eternal. I couldn't then say, *"Well, the word 'lasting' means 'eternal'"*—and try to import that meaning into other sentences that use the word "lasting." That would be inappropriate and would lead to erroneous interpretations. Spicy food may cause a "lasting effect" for some—but that doesn't mean it's eternal!

So, the word "lasting," in my example above, doesn't *mean* eternal but—in the context of a specific sentence—it can be used to descriptively *refer* to what's eternal. In the same way, the word aionios can refer in Scripture to the eternal God, but we can't assume from this that the word means eternal. Ramelli and Konstan are very clear that aionios "does *not* mean eternal." So, we can't say that just because the Bible sometimes uses aionios

5. Ramelli and Konstan, *Terms for Eternity*, 238; emphasis in original.

to descriptively refer to the eternal God, that this is what the word means everywhere else—anymore than we can say that the "lasting" effect of spicy food for some people is eternal!

This is a good place to return to Greg Beale's reasons for understanding "ages of ages" in Revelation to be saying that hell is eternal. Remember this wasn't because of the meaning of the phrase itself, but because of the context. So, what's the context that he says requires this meaning? He lists a number of references in Revelation where the same words used in this phrase, "ages of ages," refer to God, his reign, etc. But this is exactly what we were just discussing. We can't say that just because these words are *referring* to something that's eternal, these words—which he admits don't literally mean eternal—*now* somehow mean eternal. And we certainly can't then *import* that meaning into the passages about the lake of fire! We just saw why this doesn't work.

Beale seeks to support this interpretation by referring to Old Testament passages that use the Hebrew word *olam*. But it's widely recognized that the word *olam* also doesn't literally mean eternal, but perpetual or enduring.[6] (We'll examine this word at greater length in the next chapter.) Beale seems to take the context of this phrase "ages of ages" in Rev 20:10 to indicate this judgment must be eternal in 14:11, and then use the context of the phrase in 14:11 to support the idea this judgment is eternal in 20:10! This reasoning is just a bit circular. He lists quite a few places where the book of Revelation uses the same words that don't actually mean eternal— or where the Old Testament uses a similar word that doesn't actually mean eternal; assumes in each place the phrase or word really *does* mean eternal; and then uses these assumptions to interpret the lake of fire passages as eternal—even though he acknowledges the phrase *doesn't literally mean eternal*. I think it's easy to understand why someone might view this argument as tenuous and unconvincing.

The denominational leaders I mentioned use a slightly different argument. As we saw, they, too, clearly acknowledge that aionios in these hell passages doesn't mean eternal. But they still contend this word should be *understood* as eternal:

> It is true that the word translated "eternal" here (aionios) means "pertaining to the age to come." But it is precisely because the age

6. Harris et al., *Theological Wordbook*, 672–73.

to come was perceived to be without end that the word is most commonly translated in this way.[7]

But there are concerns with this assertion that should give us pause. The first problem is this contention completely ignores the many Greek-speaking early church theologians who would have strongly disagreed with this reasoning. It also ignores the actual history of how this word was translated. The writers of this book fail to mention that when Jerome translated the Greek Scriptures into Latin, he translated the Greek word aionios—which does *not* mean eternal—with the Latin word *aeternum*—which *does* mean eternal (or at least came to mean eternal). Jerome translated the Greek word aidios (which literally means eternal, as we saw earlier) and the Greek word aionios (which doesn't mean eternal, but "pertaining to the age") with the *same* Latin word, *aeternum*.

It's important for us to note again that the biblical authors and the early Greek-writing theologians we've discussed never used aidios to refer to the judgment of humanity, they only used aionios. But those who relied on the Latin Vulgate lost any sense of the distinctive meanings of these two words. The one Latin word *aeternum*, used for both, made it easy to assume the Bible was saying the exact same thing about the fire and punishment of the age to come as it was about God's power and divine nature—that they are all eternal. But the authors of Scripture used these distinctly different words in very specific ways. They used the word aionios ("pertaining to the age to come") more broadly to refer to God, the life of the age to come, and the punishment of the age to come. But they never used the word aidios ("eternal") to refer to the judgment or punishment of humanity. And neither did the early Greek-speaking church leaders and teachers.

The Latin translation of the Scriptures strongly influenced the English translation of the Bible. And English Bibles today still follow this tradition by translating the very different Greek words aidios and aionios using the same English word—*eternal*—continuing the same confusion. So, this brief assertion regarding the translation of this word seems very incomplete and misleading.

Now, I should hasten to clarify that, as we saw with Beale's contextual argument, just because the Bible uses a word to describe the eternal God doesn't mean the word itself *means* eternal. But it seems we should at least take note of how two very different Greek words—one meaning eternal and one not—became translated by one Latin word that came to mean eternal,

---

7. Free Church, *Evangelical Convictions*, 250.

and now by one English word: "eternal." This is a loss of meaning, a loss of clarity, and it has contributed to a misunderstanding of Scripture.

How did the original Greek-speaking authors and readers of Scripture understand the connotations of aionios? What did this mean to *them*? Would they have shared the perception of this future age being endless? We might think twice about being so insistent the age to come must be eternal when Eph 2:7 points forward to "the coming *ages*," and Revelation speaks of "ages of ages." If there are still age*s* to come, it stands to reason the next age isn't eternal.

But let's assume this perception is correct, and the age to come is eternal. Even if this age is eternal, can we then insist that everything occuring *in* the age to come must *also* be never-ending? Here's an important question to consider: Could it be possible the age to come itself doesn't end, but that the punishment of the lost, happening during this endless age, lasts only for a set period of time? Isn't this a perfectly natural interpretation? If so, it would be inappropriate to assume that just because the *age* is eternal, the *punishment* in the age to come can never end. If a chemistry class lasts all semester, that doesn't mean you have to spend all semester memorizing the periodic table!

Just because the *age* is eternal, doesn't mean anything that occurs within that age must also be eternal. Scripture uses the word aionios to tell us the punishment and life of which Jesus speaks occur in the age to come. We can perceive the age to come as eternal. That's fine. But to then insist that because *we* perceive the age to come as eternal whatever occurs in that age must also be eternal is reading our own speculation into the text of Scripture. And then to use this *assumed* meaning to insist on belief in eternal conscious punishment is to, once again, slip into circular reasoning—assuming our belief, reading it back into a passage of Scripture, and then trying to use the Scripture passage to prove our belief.

When someone explains that the word aionios (used in the hell passages in Scripture) doesn't actually mean eternal but instead means "pertaining to the age to come," this isn't some fringe view. It's actually in harmony with the most current and most complete scholarship regarding the meaning of the word. Interestingly—going back to the last chapter—it also reflects the divergence between the many Greek-speaking leaders in the early church and their Latin-speaking brethren.[8] So, this meaning of aionios as "pertaining to the age" is confirmed by both the latest research

---

8. Ramelli, *Larger Hope*, 105–8.

and by the understanding of the Greek-speaking teachers of the ancient church.

When I was first encountering this idea that aionios doesn't mean eternal but "pertaining to the age," I kept looking for some Bible scholar insisting, *"No, this word absolutely means eternal."* I didn't find any. There were certainly scholars and teachers who believe in eternal conscious torment. But as much as they may claim to see this view in these passages, none of them will confidently assert that this key word *means* eternal. This reluctance itself serves as another confirmation of what we're hearing from virtually everyone regarding the meaning of this word. It simply doesn't mean eternal, no matter how entrenched our traditional understanding might be.

Drawing from what we learn from the early church and from current evangelical scholars, it seems clear we should understand passages such as Matt 25 to be referring to "the life of the age to come" and "the fire" or "punishment of the age to come." This fits the meaning of the word as we've confirmed, and it fits the context. This means it would be inappropriate to use these passages to try to prove or establish the eternal conscious torment view of hell.

But some say, "Wait a minute. Matthew 25 is speaking of both the punishment of the lost *and* the life we receive as believers in Christ. If the life is eternal, then the punishment must be as well. And if the punishment *isn't* eternal . . . *then neither is the life."* (Greg Beale and the EFCA theological leaders make this argument and, I admit, I have, as well.)

At first this sounds quite logical and convincing. But let's think about it. This verse is referring to both punishment and life, and it uses the same word to describe both. So, whatever *this word* is saying about one it's also saying about the other. It doesn't mean that *everything* that's true of one is also true of the other; it just means that whatever aionios means about punishment it also means about life. If aionios means that the punishment is torment, then it would also be saying the life is torment; if aionios means the punishment is eternal, it would also be saying the life is eternal. What aionios is saying about one, it's also saying about the other. There's no way around that. The question is: What does this word aionios mean?

Since—as virtually everyone seems to be acknowledging—the word aionios in this verse means "of the age to come," then this verse *isn't addressing the duration of either the punishment or the life at all.* It's not saying *anything* about how long either last; it's saying something else entirely about both. This means that to insist that the punishment mentioned must be eternal because the life is eternal is simply erroneous, in the same way that insisting that the life mentioned must be torment because the punishment is torment would be erroneous. This verse isn't talking about the *duration* of either the punishment or life anymore than it's talking about their *temperature*!

It's completely understandable that non-scholars would make the kind of challenge we just considered. (By the way, we have many other passages that tell us the life to come is, in fact, never-ending. We don't need this passage to establish this truth.) What's alarming is to see respected scholars make the same kind of argument when they should recognize this is not really very good reasoning, and that, after careful consideration, the argument actually proves to be specious.

The word aionios doesn't mean eternal (as most seem to acknowledge). So, it's completely improper to import this meaning of "eternal" into this verse when it's not what the Scripture is saying *in this verse* about either punishment or life. We want to humbly hear what *Jesus* was saying about this life and this punishment. The divinely inspired Scripture records Jesus speaking of this fire, punishment, and life using the word aionios, meaning these all have to do with the age to come. We're certainly free to discuss the implications of what he said and any logical necessities, but it's completely inappropriate for us to read our perceptions of these implications back into what *Jesus* said in the text of Scripture—and then somehow use these passages to try to establish a view the text isn't even talking about!

Okay, so what about the Rev 14 passage that talks about the smoke of their torment rising "for ever and ever"? What *does* it mean? As Beale pointed out in the quote we read, this Greek phrase would literally be rendered unto or into "the ages of ages." This kind of phrase should be familiar to us from similar ones such as "the holy of holies," "King of kings and Lord of lords," etc. This was a familiar Hebrew way of indicating the ultimate example of something. The holy of holies is also known as the "Most Holy Place." Jesus is not just over all other kings; he is the quintessential King. In Revelation, John continually uses very Hebrew-style words and phrases, so this phrase "the ages of ages" sounds right at home in this book. Whatever he's describing with this phrase is occurring in the ultimate or quintessential ages. (This compares well with Eph 2:7, quoted earlier, speaking of what will occur "in the coming ages.") This verse in Revelation describes the *timing* of what is happening, not that it's unending. We also need to be careful about basing too much on the description of this verse because it is, as Beale also reminds us, highly figurative, not literal.

It's worth noting that we see this same Greek phrase in 1 Tim 1:17. For this verse, the ESV helpfully gives us a footnote regarding this phrase: "Greek *to the ages of ages*." It's curious that the ESV provides such a note for 1 Tim 1:17 but not for Rev 14:11 or 20:10 when it's the same exact Greek phrase used in all three. Regardless, aionios doesn't mean eternal (in either passage), so repeating it in this phrase doesn't somehow make it mean eternal or forever. Scholars such as Greg Beale helpfully show us that this verse doesn't literally mean "forever and ever."

So, putting this all together, what does it mean for us? It means these passages in Scripture that are so familiar to us, referring to "eternal" fire and "eternal" punishment are actually speaking of the fire (likely referring to judgment) of the age to come and the punishment of the age to come. This is what the word means, and I don't find anyone really contesting that. So, this would mean these verses aren't telling us anything about the duration or final outcome of hell, and—much to our surprise—they aren't teaching the idea of eternal conscious torment.

Does this disprove the idea of eternal conscious torment? No, it doesn't. Having a more clear understanding of these passages doesn't necessarily mean the eternal conscious torment view of hell is wrong. But it does weaken the biblical case for this view *considerably*. What most of us (including me) have understood to be the unequivocal wording of Scripture is at the very best highly debatable, and much more likely it's decidedly incorrect. This makes better sense of the number of Greek-speaking scholars and leaders in the early church who held views of hell other than eternal conscious torment, as we saw in the last chapter. It's difficult to understand how they could have believed something else about hell if aionios meant "eternal."

So, we find ourselves asking a surprising question at this point: *Does this leave any biblical reasons for believing in an eternal hell?* We next need to consider other biblical passages used to support this view. Are there other verses that teach us that hell is eternal? That's what we'll seek to find out as we turn to the next chapter.

Chapter Six

Do Other Passages Teach Eternal Conscious Torment?

As I MENTIONED BEFORE, whenever I had cause to explain or defend the idea of eternal conscious torment, I always relied on two foundational claims:

1. that the unequivocal wording of Scripture teaches the eternal conscious torment of the lost.

2. that this belief has been consistently held by the vast majority of the church throughout our history.

We've seen in the last two chapters that both these claims are weak, if not outrightly incorrect. We first discovered we don't have any evidence of an overwhelming consensus regarding the nature of hell in the first five hundred years of church history. And a claim that the eternal conscious torment view was predominant in the early church is particularly suspect. Significant, biblically orthodox Christian leaders have held other views of hell throughout much of the history of the church.

In the last chapter, we took a closer look at the Greek word aionios and found it does *not* mean "eternal," but "pertaining to the age" or—in the context of the hell passages—"of the age to come." So, the Scriptures that seem to speak of "eternal fire" or "eternal punishment" are more accurately referring to the fire of the age to come or the punishment of the age to come (and the life of the age to come). It's obvious this understanding strongly diminishes the biblical case for eternal conscious torment. But are there any *other* passages that explicitly teach this view? Let's look at some other Scriptures that people sometimes use to support the idea of eternal conscious torment.

Luke 16:19–31: Lazarus and the Rich Man

Whenever there's a discussion about hell, someone will invariably refer to this familiar story. So, let's take some time to think about it. Here's the Scripture:

> There was a rich man who was dressed in purple and fine linen and lived in luxury every day. At his gate was laid a beggar named Lazarus, covered with sores and longing to eat what fell from the rich man's table. Even the dogs came and licked his sores.
>
> The time came when the beggar died and the angels carried him to Abraham's side. The rich man also died and was buried. In Hades, where he was in torment, he looked up and saw Abraham far away, with Lazarus by his side. So he called to him, "Father Abraham, have pity on me and send Lazarus to dip the tip of his finger in water and cool my tongue, because I am in agony in this fire."
>
> But Abraham replied, "Son, remember that in your lifetime you received your good things, while Lazarus received bad things, but now he is comforted here and you are in agony. And besides all this, between us and you a great chasm has been set in place, so that those who want to go from here to you cannot, nor can anyone cross over from there to us."
>
> He answered, "Then I beg you, father, send Lazarus to my family, for I have five brothers. Let him warn them, so that they will not also come to this place of torment."
>
> Abraham replied, "They have Moses and the Prophets; let them listen to them."
>
> "No, father Abraham," he said, "but if someone from the dead goes to them, they will repent."
>
> He said to him, "If they do not listen to Moses and the Prophets, they will not be convinced even if someone rises from the dead."

If we look to this passage to tell us what hell is like, we immediately run into a problem. The story Jesus tells in this passage *isn't describing hell*—it's about *Hades*, or "the grave." This Scripture isn't talking about the fate of the lost after resurrection and judgment, it's merely depicting two people who have died. So, this story actually tells us nothing about hell. But, since this passage always comes up in this kind of conversation, let's consider it anyway.

Many accept this story as either describing something that literally happened or at least providing a faithful explanation of the nature of the afterlife. But some Bible scholars would caution us to be careful in how we draw insights from this story. Why? Because they understand the historical context. This story Jesus tells is noticeably similar to a folk story common in the Jewish culture at that time, but with some striking differences.[1] The way they told this story, the rich man was always the hero. The Jewish people of that time typically associated wealth with the blessing and favor of God. So, this was a moral tale intended to contrast the responsible, godly rich man with the lazy, sinful beggar. And they used what they culturally understood about Hades as the setting for this story.

Jesus uses this familiar motif, but he turns it on its head. It's Lazarus, the poor beggar, who enjoys the blessings of paradise after he dies, and it's the rich man who experiences the anguish of judgment! This would have been a shocking reversal to the people hearing Jesus' story—especially to the Pharisees.

Some would readily acknowledge this historical context, but still insist Jesus is describing something that actually occurred. And why do they come to this conclusion? Because Jesus gives us the *name* of Lazarus. We don't see any other place where Jesus includes someone's name in a parable, so—the thinking goes—this must not be a parable; it must be a literal account.

But while it's true Jesus does name Lazarus, and this *is* unusual in a parable, this claim also completely misses the reason *why* Jesus gives us the name of this character. Let me ask you: What was the rich man's name? Jesus never tells us. Think about that. This rich man would have occupied a place of prominence in his community and in the life of the Jewish people. But—in this story—the man dies nameless, just some generic rich guy, with no identity or legacy. And the person they would have thought of as a nameless, faceless, completely forgettable, poor beggar—*he* is given a name, an identity. The contrast is dramatic and would have added to the shocking impact to those hearing the story. Jesus is honoring the poor beggar in the story, and humbling the rich man. The naming of Lazarus is an integral part of the parable.

1. Keener, *Bible Background*, 224; Garland, *Luke*, 675.

But—others might say—surely Jesus wouldn't tell a story that doesn't correspond to reality, even if it was intended to be a parable. So, they would say, even if this is a parable, it must tell us about the reality of the afterlife. But Jesus often included elements of parables that, though understandable, differed significantly from actual reality. (Sowers would never have scattered their seed everywhere indiscriminately; no one would actually begin plowing and then not look where they were going, etc.) And it's quite common for teachers to utilize folk tales that aren't literally true as illustrations, as long as the people they're teaching know they're folk tales. Imagine a pastor in a church beginning a story with: *"So, these three people die, and they each go to Saint Peter at the pearly gates . . ."* Would anyone listening to this assume that this evangelical pastor is affirming the theological idea that when we die we're each interviewed at the "pearly gates" of heaven by Saint Peter?! Of course not. They would understand the pastor was using a familiar scenario as an illustration to make a point. And Jesus was doing much the same thing.

So, why exactly *was* Jesus telling this parable? As we've seen, this account was a common folk story of the day. They used it to reinforce the idea that personal wealth equals the favor of God, and poverty means someone is *not* favored by God (and likely morally deficient). But Jesus co-opts this story and turns it completely upside down, making the insignificant poor beggar the hero of the parable. Jesus was directly questioning their deeply held theological and sociological assumptions, dramatically challenging them to consider another way of thinking about life (and people).

But, still, this story does speak of two different fates for those who die. *Could* it be teaching us something about the nature of hell and judgment— or at least what death (the grave, or Hades) will be like? If we try to use this story to tell us what the afterlife is like, to be consistent we have to also accept and apply the *other* insights this passage is—apparently—teaching us. For instance, according to this story:

- How is heaven or paradise characterized? With whom is it associated? With God? Jesus? No . . . with Abraham! If what happens to the rich man is intended to describe to us the nature of hell, then Abraham is somehow the identity of and key figure of authority in heaven! Ask yourself this question: Does this emphasis of Abraham as central to heaven or paradise best fit a *biblical understanding* of heaven? Or is it more in tune with a first-century Jewish *folk understanding* of paradise?

- Just what determines who ends up on which side of the chasm in this story? The account says nothing about faith in Christ. In fact, it doesn't mention faith at all! If this story is supposed to teach us about hell (and heaven), then who goes to heaven? Poor people! And who goes to hell? Rich people! Does that sound right to you? (Some of you might be thinking: *"Yes!"*) Of course, someone could respond: *"No, it's not about being rich or poor. It has to do with the way they treated others."* Okay, fine. So, that would mean their *works* determine whether they go to heaven or hell . . . right? Lazarus was saved *because of his own righteousness*?

No, if we try to understand this story as a literal depiction of hell, for the purpose of preserving belief in eternal conscious torment, we end up with some very problematic theological baggage. It makes much more sense that Jesus was using a common folk story of the time to challenge the moral and spiritual assumptions of the people, just as many Bible scholars tell us. Regardless, as we observed before, this story is about Hades or the grave, not hell. So, it doesn't tell us anything directly about the fate of the lost after judgment.

Mark 9:43–48: "Where Their Worm Does Not Die and the Fire Is Not Quenched"

> If your hand causes you to stumble, cut it off. It is better for you to enter life maimed than with two hands to go into [Gehenna], where the fire never goes out [NASB and most other translations: "into the unquenchable fire"]. And if your foot causes you to stumble, cut it off. It is better for you to enter life crippled than to have two feet and be thrown into [Gehenna]. And if your eye causes you to stumble, pluck it out. It is better for you to enter the kingdom of God with one eye than to have two eyes and be thrown into [Gehenna], where
>
>> "the worms that eat them do not die,
>> and the fire is not quenched."

In a passage where Jesus is speaking of Gehenna (remember we explored the meaning of Gehenna in chapter 3), Jesus quotes this reference from Isaiah: *"Their worm does not die and the fire is not quenched"* (Isa 66:24). Some people would assume this worm is somehow speaking of the immortal soul of the lost, even though there's no other place in Scripture where "worm" is a metaphor for one's soul or spirit. This is a curious interpretation without any real reason for us to accept it. Others might say that, no, the "worm" doesn't represent the spirit of someone who is lost, but whatever is occurring in this passage is happening to the souls of those who have rejected Christ.

But even this interpretation isn't plausible when we take the time to look at the verse Jesus is quoting (from Isa 66:24), where the passage is poetically describing the fate of those who would be judged, and what happens to their *physical* bodies.

> And they will go out and look on the dead bodies of those who rebelled against me; the worms that eat them will not die, the fire that burns them will not be quenched, and they will be loathsome to all mankind.

This passage in Isaiah is describing the decay and consumption of physical, mortal corpses, not spirits or souls. The NIV quoted earlier makes this clear when it speaks of "the worms that eat them." The NLT's rendering of Mark 9:48 is even more frank, referring to these worms eating these corpses as "maggots."

When we look at what Jesus is actually quoting, it's difficult to read into this the idea of anyone's immortal soul. It actually strengthens the interpretation that Jesus is following the same understanding of Gehenna we see consistently in the Old Testament, and using this to warn of the coming judgment of Jerusalem in AD 70 (as we saw in chapter 3). For a Jewish person to not be buried after death, but to have their corpse subjected to such a shameful end, would have been horrific.

But what of this unquenchable fire? The NASB translation of this in Isa 66:24 gives the sense of the Hebrew here: "And their fire will not be extinguished." Let's make sure we're thinking about this according to the original context to which Jesus was referring. Isaiah is speaking of the destruction of literal corpses, which will horrify those who see what happens to these rebellious people. (The NLT reads: "All who pass by will view them with utter horror.") Many descriptions of judgment in the Old Testament include the idea of everyone looking with revulsion at the awesome judgment of God.

So—are these corpses still being eaten by maggots somewhere today? No, they're not. Is this fire still consuming their bodies? No, it's not. So, what exactly is this saying? Simply that this is the judgment of God, and no one else can *quench* or *extinguish* the fire of God's judgment. It will burn until it accomplishes God's will. It is "unquenchable," not meaning that it will never go out, but that *no one else can quench it.* (If Captain Kirk begins an "unstoppable" auto-destruct sequence, that doesn't mean it will go on forever, just that no one else can stop it!)

So, just when was this prophecy in Isaiah fulfilled (or when will it be fulfilled)? To answer that question would take us way beyond the scope of this book! But there's nothing in the words in this passage in Isaiah or the one in Mark that points to these being anything but literal corpses that are being consumed by scavengers and fire. Even if we were to take this as some kind of picture of hell, it would only be saying that no one can quench or extinguish God's judgment. God's judgment can't be stopped by anyone else; it will accomplish what he intends. All Christians agree on this.

Daniel 12:2: "Shame and Everlasting Contempt"

> Multitudes who sleep in the dust of the earth will awake: some to everlasting life, others to shame and everlasting contempt.

This is a significant passage because it's the only place in the Old Testament where we see an unambiguous reference to resurrection, people who were dead being brought back to life. But this verse also shows up in discussions about the nature of hell. This is because of the different fates for those who are resurrected, and the mention of "everlasting" contempt or disgrace. That's not quite a description of eternal conscious torment, but it is apparently a distinction between "everlasting life" and "everlasting contempt." What are we to make of this?

I was interested to see the Hebrew word translated "everlasting" here is the word *olam* (which we also encountered in the last chapter). This caught my attention because I was already very familiar with this word. Long before I was doing serious study regarding the nature of hell, I wrote a blog post on Christians and the Old Testament law.[2] In the ensuing comment thread, the issue of the Sabbath became a point of contention. Some would quote a verse such as Exod 31:16 (ESV):

> Therefore the people of Israel shall keep the Sabbath, observing the Sabbath throughout their generations, as a covenant forever.

2. Parton, "Ten Commandments."

You can see why some people would cite this verse. It clearly seems to be saying the observation of the Sabbath is to last "forever." But I had to explain that the word *olam*—in a way that's similar but not identical to the Greek word aionios—doesn't literally mean "forever." It's primary meaning is closer to "lasting" or "continual." This can be confirmed by study aids such as the *Theological Wordbook of the Old Testament*. This Hebrew dictionary explains that, even though it's sometimes translated "forever," the Hebrew word *olam* does not in itself contain the idea of endlessness.[3]

We can see this by comparing translations. For instance, the NIV translates Exod 31:16 this way:

> The Israelites are to observe the Sabbath, celebrating it for the generations to come as a lasting covenant.

This isn't an isolated example. There are many references in the Old Testament law that were traditionally rendered "This shall be a statute forever," that more current translations now more accurately clarify as a "perpetual law" or "permanent law." And we need to understand that "permanent" doesn't necessarily mean eternal. If a temporary worker is brought on staff as a "permanent employee," it doesn't mean they'll have their job for eternity!

We can see why the traditional rendering doesn't make sense in passages such as Exod 21:5–6 where a slave can decide he doesn't want to be freed from his master but he "shall be his slave forever" (ESV). Will this person actually be a slave to his master *forever*? Of course not. That's why most current translations render this more accurately that the slave will serve his master "for life." Another example is Gen 49:26 where it speaks—depending on the translation—of either "the eternal hills" (are any hills eternal?), or of the "age-old" or "ancient" hills. This is also why we need to be careful with such passages as Isa 34:10 that says the smoke of Edom "shall go up forever" (ESV). Can we see the smoke of Edom still going up? No, we cannot. And translations such as the NET translate this word more accurately as the smoke "will ascend continually."

When it's widely understood that the Hebrew word *olam* doesn't literally mean everlasting (despite its traditional rendering), but "lasting" or "continual," it would be very inappropriate to try to use this passage to somehow prove that hell is eternal. The most we could say regarding this passage in Daniel is that it's referring to some kind of lasting or continual

3. Harris et al., *Theological Wordbook*, 672–73.

contempt or disgrace. To argue anything beyond this would be circular reasoning. (Of course, if someone wants to insist that this contempt or disgrace is "everlasting," they should be observing *all* the Old Testament Jewish laws because they, too, would be "everlasting"!) If one already believes in eternal conscious torment, then it would be natural to see the "contempt" in this verse in that light. But there's nothing in this passage on which to *base* such a view.

Hebrews 9:27: "Destined to Die Once, and after That to Face Judgment"

When we've had group studies and discussions about the differing views of hell, someone will always bring up verses in Scripture that explicitly mention hell or judgment. And they'll do this with great confidence and gravitas, as if this completely settles the issue. But we can't forget that *all* of the views that evangelicals hold regarding the nature of hell include the judgment of God and a very real hell. Showing references to hell or judgment in Scripture doesn't do anything to disprove any of the other views. (Just as showing that personal faith in Jesus Christ is necessary for salvation doesn't do anything to disprove the view of universal salvation, because evangelical universalists also insist we must all be saved through faith in Christ.)

Some will use Heb 9:27 to argue there is no possible opportunity to be saved after death. Let's look carefully at what the text actually says (and what it doesn't say):

> Just as people are destined to die once, and after that to face judgment, so Christ was sacrificed once to take away the sins of many.

Hopefully you can see the problem. This verse says we'll all die once. So, this could be a good verse to counter something like reincarnation. And it also tells us that after death we'll all face judgment. So far, so good. We all agree on this. But what happens after judgment? Is there any chance of repentance and restoration? The text doesn't say. It doesn't address at all what happens after judgment. So, if we try to use this passage to argue what happens—or what *can't* happen—after judgment, we're reading this *into* the text. (This is what Bible scholars call "eisegesis," reading our meaning *into* the text of Scripture rather than drawing it *out from* the text of Scripture, which is "exegesis.") We're so locked into the idea there's no chance of salvation after death, we're shocked when we realize the Scriptures never clearly tell us this at all! To use this passage to teach one particular view of hell would be like saying that after conception comes the birth of the child—and this somehow confirms my views about parenting!

After looking at each of these Scripture passages, we have to conclude that none of them clearly teach the eternal conscious torment of the lost. So, is there anywhere the Bible explicitly and unambiguously articulates the idea of eternal conscious torment? I can't find anyplace. Does this mean hell isn't eternal? Not necessarily. We still need to look at the broader theological arguments. But it does mean my previous understanding that eternal conscious torment is an inescapable teaching from the clear and unequivocal wording of Scripture is simply not true.

The case supporting eternal conscious torment from the explicit texts of Scripture is decidedly lacking. But are there convincing theological arguments that those who haven't placed their faith in Christ will be lost eternally? We'll look at this next.

Chapter Seven

Considering the Theological Case for Eternal Conscious Torment

WE'VE LOOKED AT THE background for beliefs regarding hell. We've also examined what can be drawn directly from the explicit wording of Scripture. We've seen that the biblical case for eternal conscious torment is surprisingly *much weaker* than most of us would have thought. But there's still more for us to explore.

There are important beliefs we hold as Christians that aren't spelled out clearly in the direct wording of Scripture. Our belief in a triune God, for instance, is certainly based on what we learn about God in the Bible. But we can't point to any one passage of Scripture that gives us a detailed explanation of the Trinity. Instead, we draw together what we know from studying all the various passages that speak to the nature of God. We see in Scripture that the Father is God, the Son is God, and the Holy Spirit is God. The Bible teaches us the Father, Son, and Holy Spirit are personally distinct, even in loving *relationship* with one another, and yet God is one. Over the centuries, Christians have carefully thought through how these biblical understandings all fit together, and they've expressed this as belief in what we call the Trinity.

We all come to these kinds of *theological* conclusions about beliefs that aren't spelled out explicitly in Scripture. We want to make sure our theological conclusions—regarding the triune nature of God, for example—are solidly built on what the Scriptures actually teach, and that they're very much in harmony with the rest of the Bible. Even when Scripture does give us more explicit detail concerning a particular belief, we still strive to think deeply about what these details mean in their biblical context, and how they fit into the larger story of the Bible and the plan of God. This is what I mean by the "theological case" for these views concerning the nature of hell.

We didn't find a very convincing *exegetical* case for this view—that is, drawing from the clear, explicit wording of Scripture. But are there broader *theological*, "big picture," reasons why eternal conscious torment is true or even necessary? We're going to consider and examine the most common theological arguments presented for this view. Now, every individual who believes in eternal conscious torment may not accept each one of these arguments, and some of these ideas may overlap to some extent. But we're going to look at the claims that people most often make to contend for this traditional view of hell. So, what are the theological arguments for eternal conscious torment? Here are the ones I've found to be most common:

"The justice of God requires eternal punishment."

This is a claim we hear often, and it can certainly seem compelling. People remind us of horrors perpetrated by someone such as Adolf Hitler or Jeffrey Dahmer. We could add to this list more commonly vile offenses such as those who abuse children or extort the savings of the elderly. It can resonate with us when we hear people insist: "*Should these people really not experience punishment for these heinous sins?* After committing such horrific, unthinkable atrocities against others, should *their* suffering be alleviated? Should they just get off scot-free? Justice *demands* they pay the price for these sins, and God cannot be unjust!"

So, can we say these sins demand punishment? Absolutely, we can! There are consequences to sin, and these consequences don't just go away. But what about us? Do *our* sins demand punishment? Of course, they do! So, why aren't *we* subject to eternal judgment?

Now, we can understand how someone might say, "*Well, our sin isn't as bad as Adolf Hitler's or Jeffrey Dahmer's.*" But—assuming this is true—is that why we're saved and they're not? We can be saved because we're just nicer and less rebellious than they were? And they can't be saved because they were so horribly evil?

Let me ask this a different way: If you were standing at the deathbed of Osama bin Laden, and he asked you if he could repent before God, place his faith in Jesus Christ, and receive God's grace and forgiveness, would you respond, "*No! Your sin is too heinous! There is no salvation for you*"? Of course not! We understand God can save anyone, no matter how sinful. His grace is always greater than our sin (Rom 5:20). There is *no one* whose sin is so great God can't save them. We know that "There is no one righteous, not even one" (Rom 3:10), that "all have sinned and fall short of the glory of God" (Rom 3:23). Paul goes to great lengths in the first few chapters of Romans to show that we all stand condemned before God, in need of the same salvation. Under the law no one is justified before God, every mouth is silenced, and the whole world is held accountable to him (Rom 3:19–20).

We understand all this. So, we need to recognize this has nothing to do with how sinful *we* might perceive someone to be. Talk of Adolf Hitler or Jeffrey Dahmer might push our buttons emotionally, but it's entirely beside the point. We know that—without Christ—we *all* stand condemned before God. So, we return again to the question: Why don't our sins demand that *we* be punished? And we know the answer to this question, don't we? We're no longer subject to this judgment because Christ took on himself the consequences of our sin. Salvation is all about the grace of God; we aren't saved because of our own righteousness but because of God's grace. We're able to enter into relationship with God because Christ sacrificed himself in our place. He died our death so we could receive his life.

And when did he die in our place? Romans 5:10 tells us he did this "while we were God's enemies." He sacrificed himself for us while we still would have fit the descriptions of vile, sinful, rebellious humanity we see in the first three chapters of Romans. Jesus died for the very people who were crucifying him (Luke 23:34). Christ became the sacrifice that not only atoned for our sins "but also for the sins of the whole world" (1 John 2:2).

What does this mean? It means the justice demanded because of our sin has already been completely satisfied in the death of Christ. And, if that's true, then this is no longer a question of justice. The punishment for all sin has already been meted out to Jesus. He is, as John 1:29 describes, "the Lamb of God, who takes away the sin of the world!" Everyone must respond to God's grace in faith, of course, and we all agree with this. The question is: Can Christ's sacrifice apply to those who have already died? Can people in hell still respond in repentance and faith to God's grace? And—if not—why not? This claim doesn't address this question at all. The justice of God no more requires eternal punishment for *them* than it does for *us* because Jesus bore the penalty for *all* our sins on the cross.

I understand some Christians believe Jesus didn't die on the cross for everyone, but only for the elect (those he had chosen to save). So, according to this view, Christ didn't take on their punishment, and they must suffer the consequences of their own sin. But since Jesus didn't suffer *eternally* in our place, we still can't insist God's justice requires *eternal* punishment. And many of us find this kind of limitation of Christ's atoning work (to only a chosen few) to be in direct conflict with the clear wording of Scripture. (If you're interested in reading more about this and related questions, see chapter 14: *Calvinism, Arminianism, and Universalism.*)

We also don't want to forget that those who hold other views of hell, such as annihilationism or universalism, also believe those who rebel against God will suffer in hell. They just differ on the purpose of this suffering and its final outcome. Christian universalists wouldn't agree the justice of God requires *eternal* punishment, and most would insist that *our* sin was just as deserving of punishment. The question is: Does the sacrifice of Christ on the cross atone for the sins of the lost who have died? This theological claim we're now considering doesn't address this question.

"Sinning against the infinitely glorious God requires infinite punishment."

This is another claim that strikes a chord with us. It appeals to our sense of devotion to God, our deep worship of God, and our desire to exalt him. But if we take time to think through this idea, we find it's also problematic. What exactly is the understanding being argued here? The claim is that it's not *what* a person does that makes their sin worthy of eternal punishment, it's to *whom* they do it. God is infinitely holy and glorious, so sinning against him results in infinite guilt and punishment.

Of course, this can be merely a more sophisticated and more focused version of the argument we just considered. Christ already suffered the consequences of our sin—infinite or otherwise. But what if someone doesn't accept his sacrifice for them? Does that mean they're left unavoidably with infinite punishment because God is infinitely holy and glorious?

This can sound somewhat persuasive until we consider how sin and punishment actually work. If a child sins against their incredibly patient, loving parent, does that mean it doesn't matter what they specifically *did*, it's only about to *whom* they did it? Let's say you have two children. Your daughter refuses to eat her vegetables. That's blatant, defiant disobedience, right? But what if your son not only refuses to eat his vegetables, he screams obscenities at you, throws the food in your face, hits his sister, kicks the cat, and willfully knocks over the TV as he runs out of the house? Are your two children deserving of the same punishment? Of course not. Even though they both defied you, the extent of their actions is very different. They're both guilty, but not of the same exact sins.

This isn't the way punishment works in everyday life, and it's also not the way it works in the Bible. The Old Testament law shows very different consequences for differing sins—even differing sins *against the same person*. There's a word for inflicting the same punishment on people for very different offenses. It's called *injustice*. And God is never unjust. It's simply not scripturally true that all sin against our infinitely holy and glorious God results in the same punishment. All of the Old Testament law testifies against this idea.

You may be familiar with Luke 12:47–48:

> The servant who knows the master's will and does not get ready or does not do what the master wants will be beaten with many blows. But the one who does not know and does things deserving punishment will be beaten with few blows. From everyone who has been given much, much will be demanded; and from the one who has been entrusted with much, much more will be asked.

Those who believe in eternal conscious torment will often refer to this verse to show that God is not unjust, that he doesn't indiscriminately punish people in the same exact way. They'll use this passage to speak of different levels of punishment in hell, depending on how knowingly and blatantly the lost person defied God.

This is all well and good, but it causes a problem for the particular claim we're examining. You can't have differing degrees of something that's supposed to be equally infinite for everyone. It doesn't make any sense to argue there can be variation in the *intensity* of the punishment—but the duration of the punishment, no, *that* must be infinite. This is special pleading. Either sinning against God results in completely limitless punishment in every way . . . or it does not—which would mean God's punishment does not have to be infinite. This idea doesn't fit what we see in Scripture regarding punishment or what we know of punishment in everyday life, and it's not logically consistent with other claims about eternal conscious punishment.

"The eternal conscious torment of the lost is required to bring glory to God."

This is another claim we hear fairly often, but I confess I find this one especially disturbing. Is the eternal torment of the lost *required* to bring God optimal glory? Everyone in this discussion seems to agree that what we believe about hell tells us a great deal about what we believe about God. Yes, we all agree God is worthy of infinite glory, and that everything in his accomplished plan will result in God being glorified. But are we really to believe in a God whose primary motivation in everything is to bring himself glory? Is God really that self-obsessed? Is this narcissistic picture of God really the God of the Bible, the God who sacrifices himself for his creation because he loves them? Is this the God of the cross? Or does God only love us for the purpose of glorifying himself? Is this the God we're supposed to emulate in our own relationships?

And, even if that were so, is God truly *most* glorified by the suffering and torment of his created beings (even if they are rebelling against him)? According to what many claim, this eternal torment is supposed to demonstrate God's glory and love *to those who are saved.* This is the idea: We were all hopelessly bound in sin from which we couldn't free ourselves; God graciously released us from bondage and saved us, but left the rest to remain bound and condemned; their judgment of ongoing, eternal torment is then supposed to show us how incredibly gracious and loving God is to *us,* thus bringing God glory. But does this really make any sense?

Imagine you have seven children who rebel against you and run away from home. They all end up bound and abandoned in a house that's been set on fire. They have put themselves on a path that leads inexorably to their self-destruction. So, you run into the building, graciously unbind *two* of your children and take them to safety, but leave the other five to remain in the burning house. When your two rescued children ask why you're not saving their siblings but allowing them to die, you respond, "Because allowing them to die in the fire shows you *how much I love you!* It brings me glory because it shows how incredible is my love and grace for you." Again, does this make any sense? Does this sound like the God we see in Scripture?

"There is no possibility of salvation after death."

This idea is often confidently asserted by sincere Christians. It's stated as if this completely settles the issue: *"Well, we know there's no way anyone can be saved after death."* But the first problem we have with this claim is that we don't find it anywhere in Scripture. (I addressed Heb 9:27 in the last chapter.) This is definitely an idea most of us have *assumed,* but it's just that—an assumption. And we never want to base our theology on an assumption. We certainly don't want to somehow use our own assumption as some kind of authoritative standard by which to evaluate the truth of other claims. If we're going to hold to this assertion as some kind of absolute—to the point we believe it makes other views of judgment and restoration impossible—then we need to be able to explain clearly *why* there is no possibility of salvation after death.

We're often passionately driven to share the gospel with an unsaved friend or family member when they're close to death. We have no problem with the idea that someone can be saved in the last few seconds of life (even if they're a Hitler or a Dahmer). We even use the possibility of someone repenting in those last few seconds as a possible comfort to each other. *"Who knows, God may have reached them even in the very final split second right before they died."* But—as soon as they're dead—we assume *that's it,* everything changes. *Why?* How can we be so sure? Does God no longer *love* the person after they die? Does he no longer desire that they be saved and reconciled to him? Does he no longer have any grace for this person? Is God no longer *able* to save them?

Of course, Scripture never tells us any of this. So, why should we believe this is "just the way things are"? Why do we assume God loves the lost so much and desires to save them *before* they die, but that he can't or won't do anything to save them *after* they die? Why do we assume everything is about *this life* when—from a biblical perspective—this life is so fleeting and limited, a brief precursor of the life to come? Why do we think *we* can draw these kinds of absolute red lines, when God—in the pages of Scripture—has not?

"Eternal conscious torment is necessary for evangelism."

This is a bit of a non sequitur, meaning that it doesn't actually do anything to make belief in eternal conscious torment necessary. Even if we could show that belief in an eternal hell could be *useful* in some way for evangelism, that doesn't necessarily mean it's *true*. We don't want to adopt a belief just because it seems to work; we don't want to slip into "the ends justifies the means" kind of thinking. But this is a common argument, so let's consider it.

Scripture tells us a great deal about evangelism and gives us many portrayals of people actually evangelizing, sharing the good news of the gospel with others. But we don't see anything in the Bible that shows eternal conscious torment to be a necessary component of sharing the good news. In fact, we don't see warnings about hell to be a part of evangelism in Scripture *at all*! Many of us are so accustomed to hearing fearful descriptions of hell as motivation for people to be saved—or for us to get out there and share the gospel—that it's a shock for us to realize *the Bible doesn't do this*.

We see a lot of presentations of the gospel in the New Testament; we don't see in any of this a warning that if people don't get saved, they're going to die and go to hell. (I'm not saying this idea isn't true, just that we don't see the Bible including this as a reason—or even *the* reason—to place one's faith in Christ.) As familiar as this might be to us, we never find any of the apostles asking something like: *"If you were to die tonight, could you say without a shadow of a doubt where you'll spend eternity?"* We see a lot of places where we're encouraged to lovingly share the good news with others. We don't see anyplace where Peter or Paul motivated people to evangelize because *"those people out there are dying and going to hell!"* So, this claim of the necessity of eternal conscious torment doesn't fit what we see in Scripture concerning evangelism.

It's also not true that this view of hell is necessary, or even helpful, for evangelism. Actually we find just the opposite. We see many examples in history of people who were so repelled by the idea of a God who eternally torments his enemies that they rejected Christianity, people such as Charles Darwin and Bertrand Russell.[1] If you've spent much time sharing the faith with others, you've doubtlessly experienced the same problem. The question of hell—particularly the concept of eternal conscious torment—has almost always been an issue with unbelievers with whom I've talked. This belief has actually pushed a huge number of people *away* from the faith, especially when preached in a forceful, aggressive manner. This doesn't necessarily mean it's not true, of course, but we had better be certain of

---

1. Gregg, *All You Want*, 17–18.

the truth of a claim that others find so repulsive *before* we insist on it being necessary for evangelism!

Those who come to belief in Christ because of a fear of hell often end up weak, shallow Christians, or later leave the faith altogether. We refer to this form of evangelism as "fire insurance." This way of sharing the "good news" actually confuses both unbelievers and believers. Just think of how the gospel is frequently presented: *"God loves you and has a wonderful plan for your life. But if you don't accept him, you'll burn in hell forever!"* It's easy to see how this kind of "evangelism" can become a stumbling block hindering people from coming to faith in Christ. We don't find the necessity of eternal conscious torment in the many passages in Scripture regarding evangelism, and we don't see the wisdom of emphasizing this view in the actual responses of countless unbelievers. If anything, insisting on this view of hell seems to have done great harm.

"The doors of hell are locked on the inside."

This isn't really an argument for eternal conscious torment, but it's frequently offered as a way of making an eternal hell more understandable or even more tolerable (at least as a concept). This common description of hell comes from a well-known quote of C. S. Lewis in *The Problem of Pain*.[2] The idea is that the lost in hell are choosing an existence without God—even if it requires the torments of hell—and they wouldn't leave even if they could. I admit, I've referred to this picture of hell many times over the years myself. It does make the idea of torment in hell seem easier to accept.

But there's one real problem with this familiar description. The Bible doesn't actually describe hell this way . . . *ever*. There isn't one place in Scripture where it describes judgment in hell as something people are actively choosing and which they would resist ever leaving. Instead, this postmortem torment is always seen as something *imposed* on people by God, something to which they're subjected. So, this description may comfort us in some ways, and I understand the appeal. But it's not at all in harmony with what we see of hell in Scripture. No, we have to deal with the actual reality of the torment of hell as described in the New Testament.

I don't find *any* clear biblical references or convincing theological arguments that would require belief in eternal conscious torment. That's

2. Lewis, *Problem of Pain*, 130.

a surprising realization, I understand! But we've looked at all of the most familiar Scripture passages and theological claims used to support this traditional view, and none stand up to careful scrutiny. But are there any compelling arguments for universal salvation? Is there actually a scriptural case to be made that no one will be eternally lost, but that all will be reconciled to God and restored? We now need to face that question as we begin examining the universal reconciliation and restoration view.

PART THREE

Will God Save Everyone?

Examining the Case for Universal
Reconciliation and Restoration

Chapter Eight

Is There a Biblical Case for Universal Reconciliation and Restoration?

The Old Testament

So, we've examined the reasons for believing in eternal conscious torment, and found them to be surprisingly weak. After studying what the Scriptures actually say (relying on what Bible scholars tell us about the meaning in the original languages), we found no clear and unambiguous passage we could use to insist hell *must* be eternal. Many will agree that the theological arguments supporting this view are also profoundly unconvincing. And we discovered that a great many sound, respected church leaders and pastors didn't share this understanding of hell, especially in the first five hundred years of the church.

This leaves us with little reason—other than our tradition—to believe in an eternal hell. For most of us (myself included) this is an odd, uncomfortable place to be, but this is where a careful study of the relevant biblical passages has led us. When we put our traditional view to the test and ask, *"Where stands it written?"* we simply don't find this view clearly taught in the Scriptures.

But what about belief in universal reconciliation and restoration? Is there actually a case to be made—from the explicit wording of Scripture—that God will eventually save *everyone?!* This idea sounds strange and unbelievable to us at first, but could it truly be the biblical teaching, as many have claimed? In this chapter, we'll begin examining this view. We'll start by looking into the Old Testament. Then, in the next chapter, we'll dig into some of the relevant New Testament passages.

Not surprisingly, the Old Testament is not always as clear about these things as the New Testament is. This is to be expected. We have, for instance, only one direct, unambiguous reference to bodily resurrection in the whole Old Testament. (We noted this before.) So, we can't just expect every belief to be as fully understood and discussed in the Old Testament as it is in the New. God revealed much more of the clarity of his plan to the apostles in the New Testament than what he had revealed in the Old Testament. Still, there are some very compelling passages and patterns in the Old Testament we need to consider, beginning with those that speak to the nature of God's judgment.

The Example of Jonah

As I described before, when I first became aware of evangelical Christians who believe in universal salvation I remained unconvinced, but I was intrigued. Some time after these first few encounters, I began to teach through the book of Jonah in our church. I found this Old Testament prophetic book compelling in ways that surprised me at the time. We're most familiar with the first part of Jonah's story, of course, where he runs away from God's call, is eventually swallowed by a great fish, and then put back on the right course. What happens in Nineveh is often thought of as almost a postscript to this well-known story. But I think we're in danger of missing an incredibly meaningful part of the account.

As you'll recall, God sent Jonah to the pagan, enemy city of Nineveh to deliver a very simple message of impending judgment (Jonah 3:4):

> Forty more days and Nineveh will be overthrown.

That was it. No conditions, no clauses, no *ifs*, *and*s, or *but*s. In forty days Nineveh would be overthrown—period. If someone were to suggest that maybe there was a chance God would relent and not actually overthrow Nineveh, others could point to the unambiguous wording of God's message. God had been very clear that in forty days Nineveh *would be* overthrown, and he didn't say *anything* about possibly relenting.

Of course, we know what happened. We know that everyone in Nineveh, from the king down, repented, humbling themselves before God. And God *did* relent from overthrowing Nineveh. And then Jonah responded to God in words that are amusing, troubling, and insightful (Jonah 4:2–3):

> Isn't this what I said, LORD, when I was still at home? That is what I tried to forestall by fleeing to Tarshish. I knew that you are a gracious and compassionate God, slow to anger and abounding in love, a God who relents from sending calamity. Now, LORD, take away my life, for it is better for me to die than to live.

Isn't that amazing? Jonah is telling God: *"I knew you would do this! You're so gracious, compassionate, and loving—I knew you would relent and not actually overthrow Nineveh as you said you would!"* And he makes clear this is the very reason he ran away from God's calling—because he knew God would relent and show mercy! He'd rather *defy God and die* than see him show grace and compassion to these enemies.

There's a lot we could say about Jonah's attitude (and we'll return to this later in the book), but his strong certainty about the character of God, and what God would—and wouldn't—do, is something we need to see. The compelling example of Jonah didn't make me embrace universalism, but it did challenge my thinking in a couple of ways:

- It showed me not to think *I* know completely what God is going to do, especially if I'm assuming any limit to his grace or love. We need to always accept that we don't know the whole story, that even God's Word to us doesn't tell us everything he's going to do.

- Jonah's certainty that God would relent and show mercy was very compelling to me. *Did my perception of God include less of his grace and love than this angry Old Testament prophet?!* Did Jonah have a more clear understanding that God is "eager to turn back from destroying people" (Jonah 4:2 NLT)? Why was I so sure there's a point beyond which God will no longer show mercy and forgive?

This story actually fits a consistent, broader pattern we see in the Old Testament. It's almost as if a warning of judgment automatically included an option (whether spoken or unspoken) that if people would respond with repentance, God would relent. God himself describes this "repentance clause" in a well-known passage in Jeremiah regarding the potter and the clay:

> If at any time I announce that a nation or kingdom is to be uproot- ed, torn down and destroyed, and if that nation I warned repents

of its evil, then I will relent and not inflict on it the disaster I had planned. (Jer 18:7–8)

This is such a strong pattern, God has to make it very clear when he will *not* relent, as we see in passages such as Jer 7:16, 11:14, and chs. 15–18. God makes it very clear to Jeremiah that, no matter how much Jeremiah prays and pleads for the people, God is going to judge the nation. He will not relent. But even in the places where we see that God will not relent in bringing judgment, this unrelenting judgment is itself always part of a larger pattern we find in the Old Testament.

The Pattern of Judgment and Restoration

There are intriguing passages in the Old Testament that show God judging a certain people, and then restoring the same people he has judged. The classic example of this is the account of God severely judging the nation of Judah for their idolatry and sin, but then later restoring them. What's fascinating is we actually find a similar, widespread pattern of God's judgment followed by his restoration. Look at some of these examples from the prophet Jeremiah:

> Moab will be destroyed as a nation
> because she defied the LORD. (Jer 48:42)

> "Yet I will restore the fortunes of Moab
> in days to come,"
> declares the LORD. (Jer 48:47)

> "I will shatter Elam before their foes,
> before those who want to kill them;
> I will bring disaster on them,
> even my fierce anger,"
> declares the LORD.
> "I will pursue them with the sword
> until I have made an end of them." (Jer 49:37)

> "Yet I will restore the fortunes of Elam
> in days to come,"
> declares the LORD. (Jer 49:39)

Consider what Isaiah had to say, from the Lord, about Egypt and Assyria:

> So the LORD will make himself known to the Egyptians, and in that day they will acknowledge the LORD. They will worship with sacrifices and grain offerings; they will make vows to the LORD and keep them. The LORD will strike Egypt with a plague; he will strike them and heal them. They will turn to the LORD, and he will respond to their pleas and heal them.
> In that day there will be a highway from Egypt to Assyria. The Assyrians will go to Egypt and the Egyptians to Assyria. The Egyptians and Assyrians will worship together. In that day Israel will be the third, along with Egypt and Assyria, a blessing on the earth. The LORD Almighty will bless them, saying, "Blessed be Egypt my people, Assyria my handiwork, and Israel my inheritance." (Isa 19:21–25)

This might prompt some in-depth discussion as to exactly how this prophecy will be fulfilled! But it certainly shows nations who were previously enemies of God's people, and thus of God—and who were even judged by God—but who will both become people of God themselves! And notice the pattern we see in v. 22: *"He will strike them and heal them. They will turn to the LORD, and he will respond to their pleas and heal them."* God judges these people, he "strike[s] them." And this judgment causes them to turn to the Lord. Then God responds to their pleas, and he restores them.

In Ezek 16:46–63, God compares the behavior of the nation of Judah unfavorably with the sin of Samaria (the northern kingdom of Israel) and of Sodom, both of whom had been severely judged by God. Then God says this:

> However, I will restore the fortunes of Sodom and her daughters and of Samaria and her daughters, and your fortunes along with them, so that you may bear your disgrace and be ashamed of all you have done in giving them comfort. And your sisters, Sodom with her daughters and Samaria with her daughters, will return to what they were before; and you and your daughters will return to what you were before. (Ezek 16:53–55)

Yes, even wicked Sodom will be restored! Judah itself will be restored *just as God restores Sodom*! This compelling pattern seems to show an overarching principle:

Whatever God judges, he also restores.

This doesn't say anything directly about hell because the Old Testament doesn't say anything about hell per se. But it does tell us quite a bit about God's judgment, and hell is the ultimate example of God's judgment. This pattern in the Old Testament would cause us to expect, by default, that God's judgment—however severe—will always be followed by restoration.

We've already seen there are no passages in Scripture that explicitly describe hell as eternal with no chance of restoration. But are there passages that show restoration after God's final judgment? We'll look closely at the New Testament in the next chapter, but there are some passages in the Old Testament we need to consider.

Other Passages

> For no one is cast off
> by the Lord forever.
> Though he brings grief, he will show compassion,
> so great is his unfailing love.
> For he does not willingly bring affliction
> or grief to anyone. (Lam 3:31–33)

It's hard to imagine a more clear statement than this: *No one is cast off by the Lord forever* (or indefinitely). Why not? We're told the reason why not: *"so great is his unfailing love."* God doesn't enjoy hurting people or causing them sorrow. Jonah tells us God is eager to turn back from destroying people because he is filled with unfailing love. Here Jeremiah tells us no one will remain abandoned by God. And they both ground this in the character of God. So, God has a necessary purpose in bringing judgment, a purpose that is in harmony with his love, and this necessary judgment does not mean irrevocable abandonment with no ultimate restoration.

In light of this, consider what Jeremiah writes in other places:

> The anger of the LORD will not turn back
> until he fully accomplishes
> the purposes of his heart. (Jer 23:20)

> The fierce anger of the LORD will not turn back
> until he fully accomplishes
> the purposes of his heart. (Jer 30:24)

It's not ultimately about God's anger, and God's anger is not unending; this is about God's anger *fulfilling his purpose*, accomplishing what God intends.

And underlying all of this is the love of God. We get this from these Old Testament prophets. And then we compare this realization to passages such as this one:

> For his anger lasts only a moment,
> but his favor lasts a lifetime;
> weeping may stay for the night,
> but rejoicing comes in the morning. (Ps 30:5)

Now, take some time and consider what we see described in the following passages:

> All the ends of the earth
> will remember and turn to the LORD,
> and all the families of the nations
> will bow down before him. (Ps 22:27)

It's hard to deny that this at least *sounds* like God ultimately reconciling everyone to himself.

> All the earth bows down to you;
> they sing praise to you,
> they sing the praises of your name. (Ps 66:4)

> All the nations you have made
> will come and worship before you, Lord;
> they will bring glory to your name. (Ps 86:9)

> Turn to me and be saved,
> all you ends of the earth;
> for I am God, and there is no other.
> By myself I have sworn,
> my mouth has uttered in all integrity
> a word that will not be revoked:
> Before me every knee will bow;
> by me every tongue will swear.
> They will say of me, "In the LORD alone
> are deliverance and strength."
> All who have raged against him
> will come to him and be put to shame. (Isa 45:22–24)

How certain can we be this will happen? Notice what God says in this passage from Isa 45: "By myself I have sworn, my mouth has uttered in all integrity a word *that will not be revoked*: Before me every knee will bow; by me every tongue will swear." And he tells us what *everyone* will say: "In the

LORD alone are deliverance and strength." It even says, *"All who have raged against him will come to him and be put to shame."* Who is that, if not lost, rebellious humanity? Does this not sound like repentance and confession? Of everyone?

As you consider these passages, ask yourself: *Is there anyplace in Scripture where God demands—or even accepts—worship that is not sincere, from the heart?* Isn't that specifically what God rejects in passages such as Isa 29:13 and 1:11–18? Do verses such as Ps 66:4 (which we just read) sound like the forcibly imposed "worship" of God through clenched teeth by those who remain defiant and rebellious? Or does it sound like the exuberant praise and adoration of those who have been freed from their bondage to sin and enmity against God, and now pour out heartfelt worship and praise to God because "so great is his unfailing love," a God who—through his love—turns his enemies into his friends and even adopts them as his children?!

I am, admittedly, now drawing from the New Testament, and that's where we need to begin looking. The pattern and passages we've seen in the Old Testament are surprisingly clear and compelling on their own. In the Old Testament we find a pattern of God's judgment always being followed by his restoration. We've read in these Old Testament passages that no one will remain abandoned by God, but that everyone he created will eventually come to worship him, giving him their allegiance. And we've seen that the Old Testament prophets grounded these truths in the character of God, particularly his love. But we expect the New Testament to be even more clear and explicit, so let's turn there now to see what *it* has to say about these things.

Chapter Nine

Is There a Biblical Case for Universal Reconciliation and Restoration?

The New Testament

IN THE LAST CHAPTER, we looked at what the Old Testament has to say about God's judgment and restoration. We saw that God desires to relent from judging people, that we should expect for his judgment to always be followed by restoration, and that biblical passages speak of a future time when all of God's creation will submit to and worship him. According to Scriptures we examined, all of this is grounded in God's love. If we're seeing this correctly, we should discover the New Testament expanding on this truth and making it even more clear. Some might point out—rightly—that the passages we've looked at in the Old Testament are poetic in nature, drawn from the Psalms and prophetic books. We need for these poetic references to be confirmed in more direct, didactic (that is, intending to teach) scriptural books such as the letters to the churches. Let's see what we find in the New Testament.

Romans 5:18–19

As we study through Romans, we see in 5:10 that "while we were God's enemies, we were reconciled to him through the death of his Son." This is a wonderful truth that rightly draws us to praise God for his incredible grace.

But it also prompts some questions. Who would be included in the category of "God's enemies"? Who are those in need of reconciliation? Wouldn't that be everyone? Does that mean God has reconciled *everyone* to himself through Christ's death? Or—out of all of us existing as God's enemies, in need of his salvation—does he only reconcile to himself a select few? This leaves a question hanging that needs to be resolved. But let's first make sure we understand more of what Paul is saying in Rom 5.

A few verses later in this chapter, we see in v. 15:

> But the gift is not like the trespass. For if the many died by the trespass of the one man, how much more did God's grace and the gift that came by the grace of the one man, Jesus Christ, overflow to the many!

We should clarify a couple of things in this verse (and in the rest of this section of Rom 5). First, we see here a use of the word "many" with which you may already be familiar. Paul is using "many" in an understated, rhetorical way to actually refer to "all." This is something of which scholars and pastors are very aware, and which most commentaries and study Bibles note.

Notice it says first that "many" died by the trespass of the one man (Adam). Who would this include? Who were those condemned to death by the sin of Adam? That would be all of us, right? Paul has made this very clear in previous chapters of his letter to the Romans. We all stand condemned before God and in need of his salvation.

Since the first "many" is referring to all, the second "many" must also refer to all. Paul shows this in the fifth chapter of Romans by going back and forth between using the word "many" to compare and contrast the effect of Adam and that of Christ, and then by also using the word "all" to, again, compare and contrast who has been affected by Adam and now by Christ. Again, the interchangeable use of "many" and "all" by Paul in this chapter is widely acknowledged by biblical scholars; the observation that he's intentionally alternating between these words is not debated. So, death came to all of us because of Adam, and grace overflows to all of us because of Christ.

But also notice this isn't a simple comparison of death and God's grace, as if they're equally significant. God's grace isn't the equivalent of the death that comes because of sin. It's not merely the positive that cancels out the negative of death. No, notice the *"how much more"* speaking of God's grace and how this grace will *"overflow"* to those who died because of the trespass of Adam. I like the way the Revised English Bible (REB) brings this out:

> But God's act of grace is *out of all proportion* to Adam's wrongdoing. For if the wrongdoing of that one man brought death upon so many, its effect is *vastly exceeded* by the grace of God and the gift that came to so many by the grace of the one man, Jesus Christ [emphasis added].

Verse 17 gives us another "how much more" contrasting the reality of death through Adam with that of reigning in life through Christ. In v. 20, we read the familiar line: "where sin increased, grace increased all the more." Again, I think the REB gives us the vivid sense of the Greek: "where sin was multiplied, grace *immeasurably exceeded* it." Do you see the significance of this? God's grace and life are immeasurably more powerful than sin and death. Grace *always* exceeds sin; grace *always* abounds much more than sin.[1]

So—in the context of all of this—here's what Paul tells us in vv. 18–19 (reading again from the NIV):

> Consequently, just as one trespass resulted in condemnation for all people, so also one righteous act resulted in justification and life for all people. For just as through the disobedience of the one man the many were made sinners, so also through the obedience of the one man the many will be made righteous.

Notice again the interchangeable use in this chapter of the words "all" and "many." Who are the "many" who were made sinners through the disobedience of Adam? That's everyone, right? Then the very same word is used again: "so through the obedience of the one man the *many will be made righteous*." If the many who were made sinners includes everyone, then the many who will be made righteous *has to* include everyone. There's nothing in the text that would cause us to interpret the second "many" to have a different meaning than the first—especially considering the intentionally repeated and emphasized comparisons of the all and the many throughout this section, each referring to all humanity. If I were teaching this in a classroom setting, and drew a circle on the whiteboard to show those who were made sinners, and then drew a circle showing those who will be made righteous—it would be *the very same circle*. I don't see any way around this without doing violence to the text.

But—some will say—there's only one way to "be made righteous." Paul has made it clear in chs. 3 and 4 of Romans that only those who have the

---

1. Parry, "Universalist View," 106.

same faith that Abraham had will be justified or considered righteous. The only way for us to be made righteous is through faith in Christ! To this, the evangelical universalist will respond, "Amen!" And since Paul says here that all will be made righteous, we must understand that all will come to faith in Christ. Notice he doesn't say throughout this chapter that all were *potentially* made sinners. No, all *were* made sinners, because of the sin of one man, Adam. So, he's not saying that all will *potentially* be made righteous. No, all "*will be* made righteous," "through the obedience of the one man [Christ]." Isn't this saying the same thing we saw in the Old Testament, that all will come to submit to God and worship him? But now we see more clearly this happens in Christ.

And let's not forget the contrast in v. 20, that grace always immeasurably exceeds sin. But . . . wait a minute. We need to think about this. If sin results in death for *everyone* in God's vast creation, but the grace of God only saves a *certain number* of those who have been condemned to death—possibly even a relatively small number—how is grace increasing *even more* than sin? How is the salvation *greater than* the curse? If Adam's sin affects everyone without exception, but Christ's grace affects only *some* . . . how is God's grace greater than Adam's sin?

1 Corinthians 15:21–22

This passage compares very well to the one we just examined in Rom 5:

> For since death came through a man, the resurrection of the dead comes also through a man. For as in Adam all die, so in Christ all will be made alive.

Who dies "in Adam"? Everyone. So, who will be made alive in Christ? Everyone. "*But*," some will say, "*it's only those who are 'in Christ' who will be made alive.*" Yes. All of us agree on this. But unless we find any place in Scripture where it clearly says that some will *never* come to faith in Christ—either in this age or the age to come—we have no reason to assume there are some of the "all" who die in Adam who are not in the "all" who will be made alive in Christ. Notice again what it says: "For *as* in Adam all die, *so* in Christ all will be made alive." *Just as* all die because of Adam, *so* all will be made alive in Christ.

And then we read what it says later in this chapter, in v. 55:

Where, O death, is your victory?
Where, O death, is your sting?

If a great many of God's created beings, possibly even the vast majority, remain locked in an eternal death, or are extinguished and completely cease to exist, wouldn't this be an empty boast? Wouldn't death be able to respond: *"Where's my victory? Right here! Right here in the countless number of your precious created people who I will hold eternally, with no one to take them away from me."*

Philippians 2:9–11 and Revelation 5:13

In Phil 2:9–11, we read these familiar words:

> Therefore God exalted him to the highest place
> and gave him the name that is above every name,
> that at the name of Jesus every knee should bow,
> in heaven and on earth and under the earth,
> and every tongue acknowledge that Jesus Christ is Lord,
> to the glory of God the Father.

So, let's clarify something right away. Some will pick up on the wording in the NIV above that "every knee *should* bow," and say: "Oh, this is just what everyone *should* do." But this is simply an older form of English that's saying every knee *will* bow. This is why many other translations clearly say "every knee will bow." (See, for example, the NASB.)

This passage is drawing from Isa 45:22–24, which we looked at in the last chapter. So, is this describing people being *forced* against their will to bow to Christ and confess him as Lord? Are these people bowing to Jesus under the boots of his angels? Do we see anywhere in Scripture where God requires or even accepts insincere, forced worship? (Again, read Isa 29:13 and 1:11–18.) How could a forced, insincere confession of Christ as Lord be "to the glory of God the Father"? Or is this exactly what it sounds like, every knee bowing to Jesus, and every tongue confessing Christ as Lord. And this will be every knee "in heaven and on earth and under the earth." It's hard to get much more all-inclusive than that. And don't forget that Rom 10:9 tells us those who confess or acknowledge Jesus as Lord will be saved.

If we still want to see this as some kind of forced acknowledgment, we have a bigger problem when we get to Rev 5:13:

> Then I heard every creature in heaven and on earth and under the
> earth and on the sea, and all that is in them, saying:
>> "To him who sits on the throne and to the Lamb
>> be praise and honor and glory and power,
>> for ever and ever!"

This is inarguably *not* a forced acknowledgment, but heartfelt, exuberant praise and worship. And who is doing this praising and worshiping? The text says it's "every creature in heaven and on earth and under the earth and on the sea, and all that is in them." Once more, this is going to great lengths to describe everyone without exception. Look at it again. This includes not only every creature in heaven, but every creature on earth, and every creature "under the earth" (referring to those who have died).

This description even goes so far as to include those on or in "the sea." This is particularly meaningful here because throughout Revelation the sea indicates rebellious humanity. It's hard not to see here an intentional reference to all of God's creation—including those who were previously sinful and rebellious (compare this with Isa 45:24)—now pouring out to God lavish praise and worship. And who could deny that *this* would be profoundly to the glory of God the Father?! It's hard to imagine an ending that would bring God more glory than to have *all* of his previous enemies now pouring out praises to him in heartfelt, thankful worship!

Colossians 1:20

Colossians 1:15–23 is a section of Scripture that focuses on the supremacy of Christ, the Son. Verse 16 says:

> For in him all things were created: things in heaven and on earth,
> visible and invisible, whether thrones or powers or rulers or au-
> thorities; all things have been created through him and for him.

That doesn't leave out much of anything! The Greek word translated "all things" in this verse is used seven times in six verses (sometimes translated "everything" or "all"). This is a noticeable pattern; Paul is strongly emphasizing that he's referring each time to *everything* and *everyone* that was created.

In vv. 19–20 we read the final reference in this section to "all things," the crescendo of this obvious, specific pattern regarding *all* of his creation:

> For God was pleased to have all his fullness dwell in him [Christ], and through him to reconcile to himself all things, whether things on earth or things in heaven, by making peace through his blood, shed on the cross.

As we read through these verses, it's very apparent the "all things" in v. 20 means the same thing it's meant throughout this section of Colossians: *everything that was created*. So, who does God reconcile to himself through Christ? Everyone who was created. Who does that leave out? No one.

So, let's make sure we understand what this is saying. What does it mean to be reconciled? For people to be reconciled means their relationship is restored. If we have a family member who's estranged from us, and then we're reconciled, our relationship with this loved one is restored. If a married couple is going through a difficult time and they seek counseling, but then end up getting divorced and going their separate ways—are they reconciled? No, they're not. The relationship isn't restored. In fact, the term often used in these situations is "irreconcilable differences," right? If two Christians have been openly hostile to one another, but now come into the place where the church meets, intentionally never speak to each other, go to opposite corners of the room, and try to not even look at the other person—are they reconciled? No, of course not. There is no restored relationship here.

So, what does it mean for us to be reconciled to God? It means we're no longer estranged, no longer separated. Our relationship has been restored. We're reunited, brought back together again. And this passage tells us God reconciles *everyone* to him, he reunites *everyone* to him, he restores *everyone's* relationship with him, not leaving anyone estranged or separated from him. We're so used to reading things like this and assuming this *can't* mean everyone it's hard for us to just see what the text of Scripture is actually saying, that "all things" in this section of Colossians consistently and emphatically means *all things*.

The Kings of the Earth in Revelation

So, is there any place where Scripture indicates people in hell actually coming to faith in Christ? We find the most graphic descriptions of the torment of hell in the book of Revelation. But let's see something even more fascinating we discover in this unusual (to us) book.[2] (I'm extremely grateful to Robin Parry for describing the patterns we're about to see. Most of what I've written in these next few paragraphs is simply a paraphrase of Parry.) Let's start with Rev 6:15–17:

> Then the kings of the earth, the princes, the generals, the rich, the mighty, and everyone else, both slave and free, hid in caves and among the rocks of the mountains. They called to the mountains and the rocks, "Fall on us and hide us from the face of him who sits on the throne and from the wrath of the Lamb! For the great day of their wrath has come, and who can withstand it?"

So, are "the kings of the earth" good guys or bad guys? They seem to be part of sinful, rebellious humanity, now subject to the wrath of God, right? Let's look at what else we see about these "kings of the earth" in Rev 16:14–16:

> They are demonic spirits that perform signs, and they go out to the kings of the whole world, to gather them for the battle on the great day of God Almighty. . . . Then they gathered the kings together to the place that in Hebrew is called Armageddon.

So, the kings of the world—good guys or bad guys? Well, since they're gathering to fight Christ at Armageddon, I think it's safe to say they're bad guys, right?!

Let's look at 17:2 (speaking of the great prostitute):

> With her the kings of the earth committed adultery, and the inhabitants of the earth were intoxicated with the wine of her adulteries.

Good guys? No, definitely bad guys. And we have another reference in v. 18:

> The woman you saw is the great city that rules over the kings of the earth.

Again in 18:3:

> For all the nations have drunk
> the maddening wine of her adulteries.
> The kings of the earth committed adultery with her,
> and the merchants of the earth grew rich from her excessive luxuries.

And in v. 9:

2. MacDonald, *Evangelical Universalist*, 114–20; Jersak, *Never Be Shut*, 165–77.

> When the kings of the earth who committed adultery with her and shared her luxury see the smoke of her burning they will weep and mourn for her.

And then we see in 19:19:

> Then I saw the beast and the kings of the earth and their armies gathered together to wage war against the rider on the horse and his army.

Is there any question which side these kings are on, or to whom they give their allegiance? It's very clear and consistent, isn't it? And we see this repeated emphasis of these kings of the earth all through the book of Revelation. They're never mentioned in a positive or even neutral context from the beginning of Revelation through this ultimate rebellion in chapter 19.

And we know what happens to those who submit to the beast, don't we? Remember what we read previously in Rev 14:9–11:

> If anyone worships the beast and its image and receives its mark on their forehead or on their hand, they, too, will drink the wine of God's fury, which has been poured full strength into the cup of his wrath. They will be tormented with burning sulfur in the presence of the holy angels and of the Lamb. And the smoke of their torment will rise for ever and ever [Greek *unto the ages of ages*]. There will be no rest day or night for those who worship the beast and its image, or for anyone who receives the mark of its name.

And we see this fate mentioned also in Rev 20:14–15:

> Then death and Hades were thrown into the lake of fire. The lake of fire is the second death. Anyone whose name was not found written in the book of life was thrown into the lake of fire.

Continuing immediately into the beginning of chapter 21, we learn of the new heaven and the new earth. In v. 2 and following we see the new Jerusalem. The descriptions make clear that the new Jerusalem *is* the church, after the resurrection and the judgment. But along with these wonderful images, we see some conflicting descriptions that can be confusing.

In v. 1, we're told that "there was no longer any sea." This makes sense because throughout Revelation the sea has represented sinful, rebellious humanity. We're also told in v. 4 that there will be no more death. This compares well with 1 Cor 15:26 that says the last enemy Christ will destroy will be death. And in v. 5 of Rev 21, God says he is making everything new!

But then in vv. 7–8 we read this:

> Those who are victorious will inherit all this, and I will be their God and they will be my children. But the cowardly, the unbelieving, the vile, the murderers, the sexually immoral, those who practice magic arts, the idolaters, and all liars—they will be consigned to the fiery lake of burning sulfur. This is the second death.

How can it indicate there is no more sinful, rebellious humanity (no sea) and then describe sinful, rebellious humanity? How can there be no more death—with death completely, finally defeated and destroyed—when there remains a second death? Is God making everything new . . . *except* for all of this?

But then we read something really shocking in vv. 23–27:

> The city does not need the sun or the moon to shine on it, for the glory of God gives it light, and the Lamb is its lamp. The nations will walk by its light, and *the kings of the earth will bring their splendor into it*. On no day will its gates ever be shut, for there will be no night there. The glory and honor of the nations will be brought into it. Nothing impure will ever enter it, nor will anyone who does what is shameful or deceitful, but only those whose names were written in the Lamb's book of life [emphasis added].

So, the city is the church, the covenant people of God, with God in their midst, heaven on earth. And nothing impure can be in the church, in this city, nothing shameful, only those whose names are written in the book of life. And into this city come . . . *the kings of the earth?* But . . . *these are the bad guys!* All through Revelation they were obviously and consistently the enemies of God, submitted to the beast. We know what happened to them—they're in the lake of fire! But here they are, coming into the city. To come into the city they can no longer be impure, their names must now be written in the Lamb's book of life. How can this be . . . unless there remains an opportunity for repentance and salvation even after judgment.

What this passage describes is impossible, unless God has also reconciled these enemies of his, these kings of the earth, to himself. And—if all of these kings of the earth and "the nations" with them repent, place their faith in Christ, and then come into the city, into the church, submit themselves to Christ, bow their knees to him, and confess that he is Lord—if all of this happens, what would be the result? There would eventually be no more "sea," no more sinful, rebellious humanity. There would be no more death. Death would be finally conquered—*by emptying it.* All creation would be reconciled to God and would be restored. "*No longer will there be any curse*" we're told in Rev 22:3. (How can it say there will no longer be *any* curse if people continue to suffer eternal death in hell, or if they're completely extinguished?) God would have made *everything* new—just as he said he would (21:5)!

We have another description of this in Rev 22:14–15:

> Blessed are those who wash their robes, that they may have the right to the tree of life and may go through the gates into the city. Outside are the dogs, those who practice magic arts, the sexually immoral, the murderers, the idolaters and everyone who loves and practices falsehood.

So, the city is the church, and outside are all the lost, sinful people. This is clear to us. This also fits well with the references of Jesus to those who are "cast into outer darkness" (Matt 8:12, etc.). We have those on the inside (us) and those on the outside (the lost). We are in the presence of God, heaven on earth; and they are outside, in the lake of fire or hell. So far, so good.

But, wait a minute . . . this passage is speaking of people who "wash their robes" and then enter "through the gates into the city." And they're doing this *after* the judgment, this is *after* those who have rejected Christ have been cast into the lake of fire, *after* the description of the new Jerusalem. This verse is describing the contrast between those *inside* the city and the lost who are *outside*—in hell. And it's *in this context* that it speaks of people washing their robes, gaining access to the tree of life, and entering the city. But just *who are these people* who somehow wash their robes and then go "through the gates" into the city? They can't be us. *We're already the city!* We *can't* be the ones now *entering* the city. We're already *inside*!

So, who *are* these people? How—after the resurrection and after the judgment—can anyone *else* come into the city, into the church? There's only one way to become part of Christ's church, and that's through faith in Christ. But this passage—showing how vile are the people on the outside—still describes people washing their robes (which must be in the blood of Christ, Rev 7:14) and entering the city, becoming part of the church! And remember what it said in Rev 21:25, *the gates of the city are never closed!* Putting this all together, doesn't it mean there always remains the opportunity to repent and place our faith in Christ—even for those outside the city, in outer darkness, in the lake of fire or hell—and that eventually all will, in fact, be reconciled and restored?

No wonder it says almost immediately after this in 22:17:

> The Spirit and the bride say, "Come!" And let the ones who hear say, "Come!" Let the one who is thirsty come; and let the one who wishes take the free gift of the water of life.

So, who are we and the Spirit inviting? I can't see any way, in context, to say this *doesn't* include an invitation to those outside the city, to those in outer darkness, experiencing the second death of judgment in hell.

When I was a teenager, a friend from work invited me home to have dinner with her family. They were Jehovah's Witnesses, so it wasn't a surprise when they invited me to join them for a study after dinner. The conversation quickly became focused on the issue of the deity of Christ, and they had some challenges I hadn't heard before. So, I went home and dragged out my "research library" consisting of three translations of Scripture, a Strong's Concordance, and a Halley's Bible Handbook. I spent much of the next few days searching the Scriptures to make sure they really did teach that Jesus is God. When I was done, not only was my confidence in this belief confirmed, but I saw the deity of Jesus *everywhere* in the Bible. I couldn't avoid it!

The more I've searched the Scriptures regarding universal reconciliation and restoration, the more I've had a similar experience. The passages I've included in these last two chapters are by no means all the texts that speak of universal salvation. And the more I've studied, the more I've come to see this hope woven all through the Bible, even when I'm not looking for it. Just recently, I was researching a completely different subject. I was using the REB translation at the time, and came across Acts 3:21. My jaw dropped open when I read:

> He must be received into heaven until the time comes for the *universal restoration* of which God has spoken through his holy prophets from the beginning [emphasis added].

I checked the Greek and, sure enough, the word here is *apokatastasis*, the same word the early Greek-speaking church leaders used for this belief. The ISV, NRSV, and Phillips translate it similarly, while other translations speak of "everything being restored" or "the restoration of all things." It was amazing to see this phrase right there in the text of Scripture in black and white. When people espouse belief in "universal restoration," they're using an expression right from Scripture.

In the book of Romans, Paul takes three chapters (9–11) to answer the question of why so many of the Jewish people weren't coming to faith in Christ. He brings all of this to conclusion in ch. 11, and, in 11:26, states boldly that "all Israel will be saved." In context, this is specifically referring to ethnic Israel. In the preceding verses, Paul repeatedly contrasts unbelieving people of Israel with gentiles who have come to faith in Christ. But then in v. 26 he says that "all Israel will be saved." Some have tried to qualify this statement to mean *all Israel who remain on earth when Christ returns will be saved* or something similar—but that's *not* what the Scripture says, and it doesn't do justice to the flow of Paul's thought. Could it be that when Paul says all Israel will be saved he actually means that . . . *all Israel will be saved?* Doesn't this answer best resolve the questions Paul began to address in Rom 9? (And doesn't this beautifully fulfill Old Testament prophecies such as Isa 45:25?)

In his final conclusion, in Rom 11:32, Paul expands this to include everyone:

> For God has bound everyone over to disobedience so that he may have mercy on them all.

This ultimate answer drives the apostle to explode with praise and worship in the following verses, overcome with wonder regarding the wisdom and plan of God.

We could fill this book with these kinds of references. Over and over again we encounter passages in Scripture that *seem* to be universal in scope, but which we assume *can't* mean that. But what if we stop explaining away the clear wording of these texts? What if we take these Scriptures to actually mean what they say? What if the universal restoration that Scripture speaks of actually is universal?

We've seen that the biblical case for eternal conscious torment completely rests on what everyone seems to agree is a mistranslation of one Greek word. This leaves us with little or no explicit exegetical support for belief in eternal conscious torment. The broader theological case for an eternal hell is also decidedly unpersuasive to many of us.

On the other hand, we've now seen an extensive scriptural basis for belief in universal reconciliation and restoration, from both the Old and New Testaments. The New Testament tell us in clear language that God reconciles *everyone* to himself through the blood of Christ, he restores relationship with *everything* he has created. We're told that the same *all* who die in Adam *will be made alive* in Christ, and that the same *all* who were made sinners through Adam *will be made righteous* through Christ. We read the beautiful descriptions of *all creation* pouring out heartfelt worship and adoration of Christ. And we have confusing, apparently disparate elements of the story in the last verses of Revelation that seem irreconcilable, until they're reconciled in the unending grace and redemption of Christ for all of his creation (even for his archenemies the kings of the earth), and suddenly the pieces all fit and the picture becomes clear. And this is just the beginning of the passages we could explore!

We compare all of this with what we discovered in the Old Testament. We saw that God does judge, and sometimes he judges severely. But he always restores what he judges. Even the Old Testament prophets expected this, and they grounded this expectation in the biblical character of God. We found that God's anger is not endless, but that it has a specific purpose, that God doesn't abandon anyone forever. And we read many clear, albeit poetic, references describing how everyone God created will submit to and worship him.

Even these brief surveys of relevant biblical passages have revealed a surprising amount of scriptural support for belief in universal reconciliation and restoration. If you're anything like me, you're probably amazed at how biblically robust the case for this view is! I encourage you to be a good Berean (Acts 17:11) and continue searching the Scriptures to see if these things are so. But we need to go on now and consider the broader theological arguments both for and against this view.

Chapter Ten

Considering the Theological Case for Universal Reconciliation and Restoration

WE'VE LOOKED AT THE background regarding our beliefs about hell, we've examined the biblical case for eternal conscious torment, and we've considered the theological arguments for an eternal hell. After weighing all of this, I fail to see any convincing scriptural or theological reasons why we *should* believe in eternal conscious torment. But does this leave us in a state of ignorance about the eternal fate of the lost? We've seen many biblical passages that strongly indicate God *will* ultimately reconcile and restore all of his creation. Are there also broader theological arguments for this view? And how convincing are they? We'll look at the theological case for universal salvation in this chapter, and consider the theological challenges to this view in the next.

Three Propositions

To help us think through how we're approaching all of this, I'll ask you to consider three ideas or claims. (I'm paraphrasing something here that was originally written by Thomas Talbott.[1]) For each of the following statements, we can find Christians who believe them. But no one believes all three. As you'll see when you read them, we *can't* believe all three of these

---

1. Talbott, *Inescapable Love*, 38.

claims. They're incompatible with each other. All of us have to reject at least one of them. Here are three propositions to consider:

1. God loves everyone and intends for each person to be saved.

2. God will accomplish everything he intends.

3. Some people will be eternally lost.

Now, one could find biblical passages that—at least superficially—seem to support each of these claims. But all three propositions can't be true. So, each of us will deny one of these claims. Calvinists will disagree with the first statement. They don't believe that God loves everyone in the same way or that he intends to save each individual person. Arminians and other non-Calvinists don't believe statement number two. They would insist that God desires and does everything he can to save each person, but his ability to accomplish what he intends is limited by the individual's free will. Christian universalists deny the third claim. They don't see any biblical or theological reason to accept the idea that some people will be eternally lost. They believe God fully intends to save each person and that he is certainly able to accomplish what he intends. Thus, he will do what he intends and will bring each person to the point of repentance and faith in Christ—even if he has to utilize hell to accomplish this.

So, we have to choose between: (a) a God who could save everyone but chooses not to; (b) a God who sincerely wants to save everyone but can't; or (c) a God who wants to save everyone, is able to save everyone, and so *does* save everyone. Do we have a God who lacks loving intent for those he's created, a God who lacks the power or ability to accomplish what he desires and intends, or a God who lacks neither love nor power?

It's interesting to listen to children argue about things they really don't understand. You may recall a familiar challenge a child will sometimes throw out concerning God: *If God can do anything, can he create a rock so heavy he can't lift it?* We understand the question is actually nonsensical. The theological claim isn't that God can "do anything," but that he has all power. Just how much power would it take to create an unliftable rock? You see, the question really doesn't make any sense.

But . . . did God create people he knew he would never be able to save? By creating individuals he knew would never come to him, did God give himself a problem even he can't solve? Did he actually create a rock too heavy for him to lift?! Did God really create people he knew would be lost for eternity—people he either chose to leave damned, or whom he knew he wouldn't be able to rescue? Or did he have a plan from the very beginning that would result in the reconciliation and restoration of all he had created? Ultimately, we have to examine the scriptural support for each of these three claims. Many of us find the first two biblically certain, and the third to be ultimately without any support at all.

The Love of God

Let's think about the character of God as we see described in Scripture. Can God ever be unholy? Is there anyone to whom God would not be holy? Of course not. God is always holy, without fail. Can God ever be untrustworthy? Could God ever call people to trust in him and then not be worthy of that trust? Absolutely not. We have complete confidence in the biblical character of God. So, can God ever be unloving? Remember, the Scriptures don't just tell us God is loving, but that God *is love* (1 John 4:8, 16). Can God ever be unloving? Is there anyone to whom he would act in a way that isn't ultimately in their long-term best interest? Because—if love is an essential part of his character and he could choose not to love someone—then why should we be confident he'll always tell us the truth, or be holy, or trustworthy, etc.? If he doesn't always love others, then why should we believe he'll always love *us*? And if we say *"because he's told us he'll always love us,"* why should we trust him if he's not consistently true to his character?

No, our first instinct here is the biblical one. *Of course* God is always loving. This means that everything God does is loving, just as everything God does is holy. And we understand that God's characteristics are not in some kind of competition with each other. God's mercy is not in opposition to his justice, or vice versa. There's no struggle between his holiness and his love. Everything God does is perfectly holy, perfectly just, perfectly merciful, trustworthy, righteous, loving, etc.

So, just as everything God does is holy, so everything he does must be loving. In the same way he calls us to be loving in everything *we* do (1 Cor 13), God is loving in everything *he* does. Even if his actions are unpleasant for us or seem harsh, we ultimately find them to be loving. This means that hell must be loving. Whatever view we hold about hell must include this unavoidable truth. If God is love, if God never fails to be loving, if everything God does is loving—then hell must be loving. Hell must be in the best interest of those who are subjected to it.

We understand that hell is the punishment of God for those who haven't placed their faith in Christ. So, let's think about punishment. This is something we understand well because human parents must sometimes punish their children. So, what is it about punishment that makes it a loving act? It's the intended outcome, right? Parents punish their child *for the sake* of the child. There may be other reasons as well (to maintain order in the family, to be an example, etc.), but what makes the punishment loving is the motivation, the outcome intended by the parent. What would constitute *unloving* punishment? Unloving punishment would be punishment that isn't done for the child at all, but simply to express the rage of the parent. Right?

We see all through Scripture that even God's harshest judgment has loving purpose. His judgment is intended to bring about change in the hearts and lives of those he judges. Hell is the punishment of the lost by God, and it's something that must be loving because this is the character of God. He can no more be unloving than he could be unholy. So, what makes the punishment of hell loving? *The intended outcome.* It must be in the best interest of those God is punishing. For hell to be loving it must be remedial. It must be intended to bring about change in those being punished. It must be redemptive.

This doesn't mean God's punishment can't have any other purpose as well. Just as with the punishment of human children by their parents, God's punishment can be accomplishing more than one thing. His punishment is very appropriate because of the incredible seriousness of sinning against a holy God. His punishment can serve as a loud warning to others, an example of what happens when someone defies the Almighty God. But whatever else God is accomplishing in the punishment of individuals, the punishment must include loving intent to be consistent with the biblical character of God. The punishment of God—including hell—must be loving. It must be in the best interest of the one being punished. It must be not only punishment, but *discipline*—intended to teach and to transform. This isn't merely some emotional appeal, it's based squarely on the character of God as clearly taught in Scripture.

We also see in the Bible the kind of love to which God calls *us*. We're to love others as Christ loved us. We're even required to love our enemies (Matt 5:43–48). Does the Bible give us an end point to this command? Does it ever describe a point when we're no longer to love our enemies? No, it doesn't. So, does God love *his* enemies? Does God ever *stop* loving his enemies? We're taught it's wrong for us to love only those who love us. But does *God* ultimately love only those who love him?

We're commanded to forgive those who sin against us. When Peter asked Jesus whether he had to forgive someone up to seven times (Matt 18:21–22), how did Jesus respond? He said not seven times, but *seventy times seven*, right? Does that mean we can count to the 490th time someone asks for forgiveness—and then refuse to forgive them after that? No, it doesn't mean that at all! Study Bibles and commentaries explain the context of this verse, that Jesus is showing how God's grace is completely without limit, and that we must follow his example. Jesus wasn't giving them some final limit to how many times they had to forgive (*only 490, and that's it!*); he was showing how silly was the idea of counting and limiting how many times we should forgive someone who has sinned against us. So, how can we then claim that God has a point past which he will no longer forgive those who sin against *him*? Is God a *"do-as-I-say-not-as-I-do"* kind of God?

And let's think about God's love for those of us who are now his, those of us who will experience heaven. Does God love us? Of course he does. We can have complete confidence in God's love for us. But what if your beloved spouse or son or daughter isn't a believer when they die? Will God stop loving your spouse or your child? How can he claim to love *you*, but not love your spouse or your child?[2] How could God claim to love you, to be committed to what is best for you, and not also love the child you love so much, not also be committed to what's best for your child?

How could God expect us to enjoy the bliss of heaven while those we love deeply are either being consciously tormented for all eternity or completely snuffed out of existence? Some would say God somehow removes the memory of our lost loved ones. But this is horrific. And how would it work anyway? Would he actually remove the memory of a spouse to whom someone's been married for sixty years? What's left remaining wouldn't be your life! This would be deception, and God does not deceive. We'll *gain* clarity in the life to come, not lose it. We will know fully even as we are fully known (1 Cor 13:12).

Some say we'll gain a greater appreciation of God's holiness and judgment and so, somehow, be accepting of the eternal conscious torment of our loved ones. But certainly we'll be *more* loving in the life to come, not less![3] If we share the heart of God, our hearts will break even more for those

2. Talbott, *Inescapable Love*, 126–29.

3. MacDonald, *Evangelical Universalist*, 17.

who are experiencing hell. And we'll be even more aware of just how horrible this judgment is. No, this will give us an even greater longing for their salvation. And even if *we* are somehow unaware of this eternal suffering, *God* will certainly be aware. Will he stop loving his lost creation? Will he live for eternity in a state of grief and mourning for those either being tormented or who were extinguished? Or will he accomplish what he desires and save all of his creation?

How can heaven be fully heaven—for any of us—while anyone remains in hell? Isn't our God the one who loved his fallen world so much that he sacrificed himself, taking on our death and condemnation, so we could all be reconciled to him and receive his life? In Revelation, Jesus is the Lion of the tribe of Judah and he's also the Lamb who was slain. Jesus will eternally be the God who was crucified, who laid down everything for his creation. Do we really believe he will come to no longer love the lost people *he* created?

The Victory of God

We know from Scripture that God will ultimately triumph over all his enemies, and the last enemy to be destroyed will be death (1 Cor 15:24–28). In 1 Cor 15:55 we have this confident challenge to death (which we also looked at in the last chapter):

> Where, O death, is your victory?
> Where, O death, is your sting?

This is the glorious victory of God over all his enemies! But let's think this through. If: (a) the consequence of sin is death (Rom 6:23); and (b) the ultimate consequence of sin, the ultimate death is either an eternal, conscious death in hell or death by completely ceasing to exist; and (c) much, or even most, of God's creation remains eternally in this state of death . . . *how exactly is God triumphing over death?* How is this victory? As I asked in the last chapter, would 1 Cor 15:55 above not be an empty challenge? Would not death be able to respond to these questions: *"Where is my victory? Right here! In the countless number of your precious creation who will eternally remain dead."* How can we say that death has been *destroyed* if anyone remains dead?

We use the term "lost" for those who aren't yet saved, and it's a biblical word. But when the shepherd leaves the ninety-nine sheep and seeks the one who's lost (Luke 15:1–7), to *whom* is the sheep lost? Who is the one in the story who has experienced the loss? It's the shepherd! And he's seeking to restore his lost sheep to *himself*.[4] When the widow loses one of her silver coins (Luke 15:8–10), to whom is the coin lost? To her! And she searches to restore the coin to *herself*. To whom is the prodigal son lost (Luke 15:11–32)? To his father! And he watches and waits until he can restore his son to himself. So, to whom are the lost actually *lost*? *To God*. And he longs to restore even the last one who's lost to himself. Will he experience eternal loss? Or will he be victorious?

Again, imagine you have seven children. And let's say your children all rebel against you and become victim to a mind-controlling cult that will ultimately destroy them. So, you endeavor to do everything you can to rescue each child you love so much from this destructive cult and bring them to freedom. In the end, heartbreakingly, you're able to rescue only two of your precious children. The other five remain, and take part in the mass suicide of the cult. Would you then exult, *"I have been triumphant! I have completely won the victory"*? Is this really the kind of victory for God that Scripture is describing?

We read in 1 Thess 4:13 that believers "do not grieve like the rest of mankind, who have no hope." This is a wonderful, blessed truth to which we hold tightly when we experience the loss of a loved one. But is this only true for our loved ones who we know have placed their trust in Christ before they died? For the rest, are we back to grieving like the rest of mankind *with no hope*? Is our hopeless grief actually *worse* than the rest of mankind because we know so well the consequences of death without faith? Or does Scripture give us hope for *all* our loved ones who die because our trust is in the unconquerable love of God (Rom 8:38–39) and his sacrifice for all people (1 John 2:2)?

In John 10, Jesus contrasts himself as the Good Shepherd, who comes "that they may have life and have it to the full" (v. 10), with the thief who comes to steal, kill, and destroy. But according to both eternal conscious punishment and annihilationism, what does God do with those who are lost? Does he not *kill* and *destroy* them? Is he not doing to them exactly what the enemy desires to do? How, then, is God victorious over Satan? Even if Satan is eternally bound, can't he go to hell with a smile on his face because he's taking so many of God's created beings with him, and even

4. Gregg, *All You Want*, 57.

seeing *God* accomplishing Satan's intended design for them: their death and destruction? How is this victory for God?

Will evil actually exist for all eternity? Will sin remain in the hearts of those in hell forever? Will God truly be utterly supreme over everything everywhere (1 Cor 15:28) . . . *except* for his rebellious creation in hell who still resist and refuse him as Lord and King? Or does he remove his opponents by *killing* them—somewhat like ensuring a unanimous vote by killing all those who vote against you?[5] Is this really the complete and glorious victory of God? Or . . . does he win complete victory over even his most hostile enemies by transforming them and making them his devoted subjects, even adopting them as his own sons and daughters, bringing them to the point of heartfelt, passionate worship?

Which View Best Fits the Gospel?

While arguing against Robin Parry's evangelical universalist view, Jerry Walls wrote:

> I will also concede that his view represents the end of the biblical story that is most to be desired. The universalist view delivers on the promise of a truly perfect end of the story.[6]

Now I have great respect for Jerry Walls, but I have to ask: How can the "truly perfect" end of the story not actually *be* the end of the story? How can *we* come up with a better end of the story than God did? Could it be that this conclusion isn't too good to be true, but that it's too good to *not* be true? As we've seen, this view isn't based on warm and fuzzy wishful thinking, but on rigorous exegesis of Scripture. And which view best fits the good news of Jesus Christ? Which best fits into the whole biblical story?

In his book examining the different views on hell, Steve Gregg tells us he's still struggling with this issue, that he hasn't definitively reached a conclusion yet.[7] I certainly respect that kind of transparency. But we can perhaps see a bit of his process in the headings he chose for the different sections of his book. The two-chapter section on eternal conscious torment he titled "First, the Bad News." The next section on annihilationism he titled "The Bad News Is Not as Bad as You Thought." And the final section

5. Parry, "Universalist Response," 91.
6. Walls, "Purgatory Response," 141.
7. Gregg, *All You Want*, 299–301.

on restorationism he titled "The Good News Is Better Than You Thought"! Again, it seems we're all wrestling with the question: How could *we* think of anything better than God's good news?

In Robin Parry's response to another view, he uses playful—but I would say insightful—descriptions of the differing views. He describes those who believe in eternal conscious torment as "tormentors," and those who believe in annihilation as "terminators."[8] Those who believe in evangelical universalism are then, I would think, "transformers." As everyone agrees, what we believe about hell reveals what we believe about God. So, the question is really: Do we believe in a God who's ultimately and finally a Tormentor, a Terminator, or a Transformer? Which best fits his character as revealed in Scripture? Which best fits his gospel? Which best fits the biblical story?

What do we see in the gospel, taking it in its whole canonical context? We see God's creation ruined and then restored. We see his people, Israel, ruined and then restored. We see us, humanity, ruined by the fall into sin, but then restored. At the heart of his gospel, we see Christ sacrificing himself, taking on the death brought by sin, in order to reconcile and restore his fallen, rebellious creation. We see the mission that comes from the gospel, the mission which we now pursue. And we see the ultimate culmination and final victory of God's plan, accomplishing what he intends to accomplish, what he accomplished on the cross. So, which understanding of hell best fits this gospel, the *eternal torment* of those lost to God, the *termination* of those lost to God, or the *transformation* and *restoration* of those lost to God?[9]

There's so much more I'd like to write about this, but much of it would get too involved for a chapter intended to be concise and easily accessible. For instance, it's been fascinating to see all the ways biblical universalism resolves so many issues debated between Calvinists and Arminians (and other non-Calvinists). If this intrigues you, I've added a bonus chapter at the end of this book that examines some of these fiercely debated issues and how they're beautifully resolved with belief in God's universal reconciliation and restoration.

There are many other intriguing insights I'd like to include here as well. In one of our church's group discussions on this topic, Chris Brackett (one of our pastors at The Orchard as well as a close friend) pointed out

8. Parry, "Universalist Response," 89–92.
9. Parry, "Universalist Response," 91.

that we believe Christ paid the penalty for our sin (because, of course, the Bible tells us this). Jesus took on our death so we can receive his life. But if the wages of sin is death, and if that death means either eternal conscious torment or annihilation, then Christ actually *didn't* take on our death, the consequence of our sin—because Christ was neither eternally tormented nor annihilated! The belief that Jesus suffered *our* punishment in our place doesn't work if we believe the punishment for our sin against God is eternal conscious punishment or annihilation; it only works if we believe in ultimate reconciliation and restoration.

It's difficult to not explore more of these kinds of insights, but I think it's best to end this chapter here. I don't see sufficient biblical support for eternal conscious torment, and I don't find any of the theological arguments persuasive. But I find many passages of Scripture that show the ultimate reconciliation and restoration of all of God's creation, and I find the theological arguments for this view deeply profound and compelling. When we frankly consider the implications of each view, when we really ponder the love of God and the ultimate victory of God as described in Scripture, and when we think through which view best fits both the biblical character of God and the gospel of Jesus Christ, I contend this leads us inexorably to God planning and ultimately accomplishing the reconciliation and restoration of *all* of *his* creation. But what of the theological challenges to universal salvation? We'll look at these next.

Chapter Eleven

Theological Challenges to Universal Reconciliation and Restoration

IN THE LAST CHAPTER, we looked at the theological case *for* universal salvation. So, now we need to consider the theological *challenges* to this view. Let's look at the most common questions and challenges we'd typically hear in response to belief in universal reconciliation and restoration.

"So it doesn't matter what you believe? You can just believe anything you want and go to heaven?"

This is often the first response I hear to this belief, but it doesn't really apply to Christian universalism at all. Universal reconciliation and restoration is definitely *not* the idea that someone can believe anything they want and go to heaven anyway. Evangelical universalists stress the necessity of personal faith in Christ for one's salvation. This is as essential for them as it is for any other Christian. But—drawing from the Scriptures—they believe that God will eventually bring every individual to the point they do indeed place their faith in Jesus Christ.

Imagine we are all on a ship at sea. Something happens to the ship, and it begins to sink. A few of the people in our group are deeply frightened there won't be enough lifeboats, or that all the passengers won't be able to get to the lifeboats in time. But an angel from God appears and assures our group that every person onboard the ship *will* reach a lifeboat and be taken to safety. Would it make any sense to then conclude, *"Well, if everyone's gonna be saved anyway, then it doesn't matter if we get in the lifeboat or not"?* Of course not! Getting in the lifeboat is the *way* the passengers and crew will be saved.

Scripture teaches that God will save everyone, and this only happens as each individual places their personal faith in Jesus Christ. The gospel is necessary for everyone. "Salvation is found in no one else, for there is no other name under heaven given to mankind by which we must be saved" (Acts 4:12).

"Then why even get saved now?"

This is another common response. And, in some ways, it can sound logical. If everyone's going to ultimately be reconciled to God *anyway*, why not just live my life and let God save me whenever? But this is actually the saddest challenge we could hear from a follower of Christ. The idea underlying this question is that we're only saved to escape hell. So, if that doesn't seem so urgent a motivation to us, then why get saved right now? That's a tragic attitude for a Christian. What's our motivation for living a life in Christ? It's *living life in Christ*! We aren't just saved to escape hell and go to heaven— although this is true—but for *so much more*. We begin to know God *now*, to experience life in his presence *now*, to live life in the Spirit *now*, freedom from sin, spiritual growth and maturity, the life of the body, etc.

Asking *"Why get saved now? Why not wait until I've lived my life?"* is like asking *"Why get married now? Why not wait until I've lived my life?"* Both of these sentiments are coming from someone who doesn't really understand how precious is the relationship they're postponing. We don't experience this life in its fullness yet, but we do experience it genuinely here and now. We never want to think lightly of the life Christ brings us into, *his* life. He sacrificed everything to give us this life. We must never diminish it this way. Why come into relationship with Christ now? To be *in relationship with Christ now*!

"But what's the big deal going to hell if you're going to get out eventually anyway?"

This is often the follow-up question to the previous challenge. But this question doesn't make any sense either when we really think about it. When faced with a forty-year term in a maximum security prison, would we shrug our shoulders and say, *"What's the big deal? I'm going to get out eventually anyway?"* If you had a choice between (a) suffering for a very long time fighting cancer, coming close to death over and over again, going through operations and radiation and chemotherapy and losing your hair, but ultimately surviving; or (b) not dealing with cancer at all—would you shrug your shoulders and say "What's the big deal?" If you knew your child could either spend much of their life bound in drug addiction and all the destruction that comes with that, but ultimately survive—or never struggle with drugs at all—would that maybe be a big deal to you?

"If everyone receives God's grace, then it's no longer a gift, it's something God owes us."

I'm surprised by how often I hear this because this, too, doesn't make any sense if we just stop and think about it. If you have four children and you give them all Christmas gifts, does that mean they're no longer gifts? Because you gave them to *all* your kids, do they somehow become something you *owe* your children? If your boss gives you a bonus of a million dollars, that would be an incredibly gracious gift, wouldn't it? And if they decided to bless *all* of their employees with a bonus of a million dollars each, does that make this gift to you any less gracious? Is it now something your boss owed you? Of course not.

"Yes, God is loving, but don't forget he's also holy."

Robin Parry shares how people will tell him this as if it's something he hasn't thought of. *Oh, yeah, that's right! How could I forget that God's also holy?* Yes, we know that God is not only loving, but also holy and just. But we must be careful to never think of his holiness as somehow in conflict with his love, or his mercy as contending against his justice. God's not schizophrenic. It's not appropriate to pit one aspect of his character against another. There is no such conflict within God, no struggle within his character. Everything he does is both perfectly and completely holy, and perfectly and completely loving. Everything he does is both thoroughly merciful and thoroughly just.

Some suggest that God's holiness is somehow more central than love to who God is. But when someone asked Jesus what was the greatest commandment, it's significant that he responded with two commandments about love: loving God with all our hearts, and souls, and minds; and loving our neighbors as ourselves (Matt 22:34–40). He said that "all the Law and the Prophets hang on these two commandments." Jesus himself made these two commandments central, on which *everything else* hangs. And what are these two commandments speaking of? Holiness? No, *love*. Jesus makes love absolutely primary for the life of the believer. Later he would give his disciples a new commandment: love one another (John 13:34–35). And how does Jesus say everyone will know we're his? By our holiness? No, by our *love*.

If Jesus himself repeatedly emphasized the centrality of love, doesn't this tell us something about God? Don't the teachings of Jesus reveal God to us, and doesn't this mean love is central to who *God* is? After all, Scripture tells us God *is* love (1 John 4:8, 16). Does this dismiss or diminish the necessity of holiness? Absolutely not. But holiness has to do with being set apart, untainted by anything that might corrupt or pollute us. We are to be holy as God is holy (1 Pet 1:15–16). Holiness is necessary, but by itself incomplete.

Holiness provides the pristine, sterile environment for healthy, loving relationship between us and God, and us and each other—but it doesn't, by itself, create that relationship. Holiness without love is like a perfectly clean kitchen without cooking anything! It's like a nursery safe from anything that might harm or destroy—but with no child. Not being unfaithful to one's spouse is right and necessary, but it only eliminates what would destroy loving relationship. The *loving relationship* is what's at the heart of a marriage.

Our God exists eternally in loving relationship. This is the very core of who he is. The Trinity shows us that loving relationship is eternally central to who God is, and so must be central to our understanding of him. So, of course, he makes this primary to who we are to be, as well. Holiness provides the necessary environment for loving relationship, but it's empty and pointless without it. The God of the Bible is *all about* loving relationship. He is a God of both holiness and reconciliation, restored relationship. He's the holy God who sacrificed himself to bring us back into loving relationship with him. This is the gospel, and it tells us *who he is*. Without understanding the centrality of love, we do not rightly understand God (1 John 4:8).

"This view doesn't take sin or hell seriously."

The person making this claim hasn't read very many Christian universalist theologians. Those who believe in universal reconciliation and restoration take sin and hell just as seriously as do other believers. They believe in and emphasize the same vileness of sin, the same anger of God toward sin, and the same judgment of those who persist in unrepentance. Ironically, it's some who believe in eternal conscious torment who try to find a way to soften the harshness of hell, saying that hell won't be all that bad for some of the people there, and they may even be almost happy in hell.[1]

The evangelical universalist doesn't have to jump through these hoops to try to make hell tolerable. We can teach that hell is torment, isolation, a place of weeping and gnashing of teeth. It's the ultimately harsh judgment of God, even more extreme than other examples of God's harsh judgment we see in Scripture. And just as the pattern we previously observed in Scripture, God's judgment, however severe it is, has an ultimately loving purpose, leading to change of heart, repentance, reconciliation, and restoration. Those who believe in universal restoration can be strict exclusivists (that is, insisting that people must be saved by knowingly and specifically placing their faith in *Jesus Christ*, not just God in some vague sense) because the opportunity for salvation in Christ doesn't somehow disappear after they die. God will save everyone, but this also means that every person *needs* to be saved—because of their sin.

"But God destroyed people in the flood, and in Sodom and Gomorrah."

Some people will bring up examples of judgment in the Bible, such as God destroying most of humanity in the flood or his destruction of the entire cities of Sodom and Gomorrah. "If God was willing to destroy them," they suggest, "then he'll have no problem destroying people in hell." And these are serious, sobering examples of God's judgment, no doubt about it. But was this *eternal* destruction? These people lost their physical lives here on earth (which they would all lose anyway), but did they cease to exist completely, or face unending torment? Remember, evangelical universalists believe in judgment, even the extreme judgment of hell. What they don't believe is that this judgment is never-ending without any hope

---

1. Walls, *Logic of Damnation*, 128.

of reconciliation and restoration. Because these examples deal with judgment in this life only—leading to physical death—this is really comparing apples and oranges. It would be like saying, *"Well, our parents disciplined us harshly, so that means they would have no problem killing us."* It's simply not the same thing. (And don't forget that God says he will restore Sodom [Ezek 16:53–55].)

"The wrath of God is necessary for God to be glorified."

In the book *Four Views on Hell*, Robin Parry wrote the chapter on evangelical universalism, while Denny Burk defended eternal conscious torment. In Burk's response to Parry's chapter, he takes issue with Parry's understanding that God's wrath is a manifestation of his love. To Burk, wrath is a part of God's character in the same way that love or holiness or justice are.[2] But this isn't a biblical understanding of God. Is God perpetually angry? Has he always been angry? Will he be angry for all eternity? Burk seems to think so:

> God does not love those who are put in hell. On the contrary, his wrath means that he is angry at them forever (Rom. 2:8).[3]

Notice that Burk apparently views anger and love as being mutually exclusive, as if God isn't able to both love someone and be angry with them. Does this ring true? I wonder if Denny Burk has never been angry with his children. And if he has been, does that mean he stopped loving them? Was God not angry with the people of Israel? Did that mean he had stopped loving them? Of course not.

Notice also that Burk references Rom 2:8 to support the claim that God is angry with the lost "forever." Let's take a look at this verse ourselves to confirm what Burk is confidently asserting:

> But for those who are self-seeking and who reject the truth and follow evil, there will be wrath and anger.

Does this verse speak of God's wrath and anger? Absolutely, no one denies that God is angry toward those who sin. But does it say here that God is angry with anyone *forever*? No, it does not. It doesn't say anything about that. Burk may think what he's claiming makes sense, but he has to read

---

2. Burk, "Torment Response," 131.
3. Burk, "Torment Response," 131.

that meaning *into* the passage, because the passage says nothing about how long God will be angry. (An assumption that would better fit the biblical text is that there will be wrath and anger for these people as long as they are self-seeking, reject truth, and follow evil.)

So, what *do* we see in Scripture about God's anger? Let's see:

> For his anger lasts only a moment,
> but his favor lasts a lifetime. (Ps 30:5)

> You do not stay angry forever
> but delight to show mercy. (Mic 7:18)

How many places do we read that God is "slow to anger"? How can God be slow to anger if wrath is an essential part of his character? Is he slow to be holy? Is he slow to love? Instead, we read that God's anger is a temporary response for a specific purpose:

> The anger of the LORD will not turn back
> until he fully accomplishes
> the purposes of his heart. (Jer 23:20)

No, Parry's view of God is much more biblical, and Burk's is disturbingly similar to the capricious, irritable gods of paganism.

Remember what we saw in the first chapter of Colossians that just as "all things" were created in Christ, these same "all things" God has reconciled to himself through Christ, "making peace through his blood, shed on the cross" (1:20). You don't remain eternally angry with those whom you have reconciled to yourself, those with whom you have made peace through your own blood. God reconciled us to him through Christ's death while we were still his enemies (Rom 5:10). This is the God who chose to be crucified in order to reconcile all of his creation to himself.

And this perpetual state of wrath is supposed to be to God's glory. But does that make sense? Would it really bring him most glory to be unceasingly angry toward much of his creation for all eternity, subjecting them to endless torment to appease his wrath? Does this picture of God really glorify him, or does it actually diminish his glory? Would it not bring much more glory for him to thoroughly defeat his enemies by transforming them into his friends, even bringing them into his family as his children, so he has no more need to be angry toward his creation? Isn't this much more glorifying of God?

"Universal salvation is a man-centered theology."

A sometimes effective manner of scaring people away from a theological belief is to accuse it of being a "man-centered" belief, something that makes humanity the focus and driving force rather than God. And there is a real danger here. The idea that *"God helps those who help themselves,"* for instance, could be called "man-centered" because it makes humans the determining element, with God a much more passive, secondary part of the picture. This is something biblically-minded Christians would rightly guard against. So, let's stop and actually compare beliefs.

Some bend over backwards to avoid anything that could be called "man-centered" by essentially taking humanity out of the equation completely, at least as far as truly determining anything. For them, God *could* save every individual—but won't. He determined that Adam and Eve would sin (because, according to them, he determines everything that occurs); he determined that many if not most people would be born with a rebellious human nature from which they could not free themselves (nor could they even want to), a rebellious nature from which *he* would not free them, and which would make their personal sin inevitable and inescapable; and so he thus determined—before they were even born—that they would be eternally condemned, with never a *chance* for salvation. This certainly can't be called man-centered! But at what cost? This is so far from being "man-centered" it takes away any loving focus *at all* that God might have for these people he created, the kind of loving focus that might make him willing to suffer in their place on the cross. This isn't man-centered, that's true; in fact, for most of humanity it's completely devoid of any truly loving intent.

Others claim that God *does* desire to save everyone, but that he's ultimately, eternally stymied by the stubborn rebellion of human beings. He wants to save them, but they say, "No!" Their hearts are simply too hard for God's love and grace to overcome. This actually does seem to be "man-centered," because it makes fallen humans the ones who have the final word contrary to God's will for them. According to this idea, some humans will have the ability to say "No" to God eternally, defying his authority as Lord and God.

Now let's look at the other belief. According to this view, God's love is unconquerable and can overcome the hardest heart (compare this with Rom 8:38–39). God's grace is always greater than sin, more powerful than sin, always surpassing sin (Rom 5:15, 20). God will not stop until he has restored to himself everything that was lost *to him* (Luke 15).[4] God's truth will expose all deception (Luke 8:17); God's light will drive out all darkness (Rev 22:5). God will be completely victorious over all his enemies, even destroying death itself (1 Cor 15:26). Show me again how this is "man-centered"?

"But what about free will? Does God force people to repent?"

This is the most thoughtful challenge to Christian universalism I've heard. What if people don't *want* to be reconciled and restored? We need to take some time to really think about this. Let's begin by assuming—for the sake of discussion—that some people just won't stop rejecting God. I'll explain later why I don't believe this is true, but let's assume for now it is. Does this mean God's hands are tied, that there's nothing he can do? Is the free will of humanity somehow the most sacred, inviolate virtue above all else? And where exactly do we go in Scripture to see that human freedom is the one principle that overrides all others?

If your two-year-old is running headlong straight into a busy street, do you place their free will above all other concerns? Or do you take immediate, decisive action to prevent them from being destroyed? (*"No!"*) We do allow children to experience the consequences of their actions when it doesn't actually destroy them. We allow them to pay the price for their free will choices so they can learn what is beneficial and what is dangerous. We may let them touch something that's hot, for instance, so they learn that hot things burn. But there's a limit to how much free will we allow them, isn't there? It's one thing touching something hot; it's something else entirely to stick their arm in the fire. From God's perspective, how much different are we than a two-year-old?

It's common for some evangelical Christians to say things without realizing how contradictory they are. For instance, we frequently say that "God is always a gentleman," that God won't force himself onto anyone. And then, virtually in the same breath, we can talk about God as the "Hound of Heaven" who aggressively pursued us unrelentingly until we surrendered.

4. Gregg, *All You Want*, 57.

And we never stop to realize these descriptions of God contradict one another.

If God is always a gentleman, someone needs to explain this to the apostle Paul who was knocked to the ground and blinded on the road to Damascus! Or to C. S. Lewis, who describes himself as being brought in "kicking, struggling, resentful, and darting his eyes in every direction for a chance of escape." (He goes on to say of God, "His compulsion is our liberation.")[5] That doesn't sound like a gentleman to me, but it does sound like a very focused parent intent on doing what's best for their child. I do find it a bit ironic that many of the same people who insist that passages such as Phil 2:9–11 can't be describing voluntary worship—that these people are being forced to acknowledge God—will then turn around and question how God could force people to repent! Apparently for these people it's okay for God to force the lost to confess Jesus Christ as Lord as long as he doesn't actually save them!

So, am I saying that God doesn't respect the free will of the lost but forces them to repent? Not at all. But we need to think about what we mean by a "free choice." As many Christians who emphasize free will have clarified, they don't so much believe in free will, as they do free*d* will. We were bound in sin and rebellion and our fallen sin nature, but God freed us, enabling us to choose, so that we could embrace him, placing our faith in Christ. For a choice to be free, it has to be . . . *free.*

Let me illustrate. Suppose a person is under the influence of a powerful drug and they attack someone. Are they responsible for their actions? We might say, "Maybe," especially if they knew the dangers of the drug before taking it. But what if someone else put the drug in this person's food or drink, and they consumed it without knowing? If they had no control at all over their behavior, then they would be deemed as not responsible for what happened. Their actions were not done by way of a free choice.

If we walked into a room and saw a young man holding his hand in a fire without pulling it out,[6] even though it was being badly burned, what's the first thought that would go through our minds? *"There's something wrong with that guy,"* right? Why? Because people don't do that—not freely. If we're doing something *that* painful, *that* self-destructive, our action *itself* is evidence that something's wrong with us. This isn't a choice we're making freely; there's something else causing us to act in this manner.

5. Lewis, *Surprised by Joy*, 279–80.
6. Talbott, *Inescapable Love*, 171–85.

Now let's think about salvation. We were created to live in relationship with God. Even in our fallen state we long for that connection. This is why throughout history humans have been drawn to religion or spirituality of some kind (or at least some larger cause than themselves). As Christians, we know that all our most intense longings and yearnings, our deepest questions, even the ones we can't express—all of this only finds satisfaction in Christ. We only find ultimate fulfillment and purpose in Christ. We even only come to truly know ourselves *in him*.

Do people reject God? Of course they do. (We did ourselves at one time.) *Why* do people reject God? We could make a list of reasons, couldn't we? Some don't believe that God exists; some resist authority; some don't like religion or have been hurt by Christians; some feel they'd be giving up too much control. So, do people have reasons for rejecting God? Yes. But are they *good* reasons? Would we say that any of these are sound, logical reasons why someone *should* reject God? No, not at all. In fact, we'd try to help the person see that these "reasons" for rejecting God are illusions, they're fairy tales. God does exist; Jesus is very different from religion; we don't really have control over our own lives; etc.

So, there is no sound, rational reason for rejecting Christ, and *every* reason to receive him. Anyone who rejects Christ, especially in hell, is not doing this freely. To refuse what you were created for and what will satisfy every longing and desire put within us by God, but to instead "choose" to remain in a state of torment and ongoing death, is not a free choice. It's an insane one, one devoid of rational thought, just like the young man holding his hand in the fire. Just as Scripture describes the lost in this life, such a person is bound in deception and darkness. The question is what does God do with this person? Does he bring the young man to the point of clarity so he understands the insanity of holding his hand in the fire and can then make the free choice to remove it? Or does he say to the young man who is bound in delusion and completely irrational, "You want to hold your hand in the fire? Fine! I'll make sure you hold it there *forever!*"

But some will say, *"Yes, it's insane and they're deceived, but that's just their nature! It's their nature to reject God; that's why they're in hell!"* But wait a minute. Let's think about this again. Yes, we all have a fallen, sinful nature, but did we choose to have that nature? Did you choose to be born into a sinful, rebellious race? No, the Scriptures are clear about this: "For God has *bound everyone over to disobedience* so that he may have mercy on them all" (Rom 11:32). We didn't choose our sinful nature. All of us were subjected to this sinful nature (so that God could have mercy on all of us). God brought each of us who are now saved to the point of clarity and freedom where we knew the incomparable greatness of knowing Christ our Lord. That's the only way we could be saved. Otherwise we remain bound in sin, rebellion, darkness, and death—not by free choice but because this was part of God's plan. We were bound in disobedience. God freed us so we could make a free choice and choose life in him—just as he intended.

The very same thing is still true of the lost person in hell. They're not able to make a free choice until God brings them to this point of clarity and freedom. Until then, they remain bound in sin, rebellion, darkness, and death—not by free choice but because it's part of God's plan. He's bound us all in disobedience so he could have mercy on us all. And, just as with many of us, it can be a long, drawn-out process to bring us to that point of clarity, freedom, and surrender. God will use anything in our lives to bring us to this point of freedom of choice—even hell.

"But isn't this torturing people until they give in? Isn't this forcing them to believe?" Not at all. Most evangelical Christians are quick to describe hell as the absence of God. (This doesn't necessarily mean that God can't be active in hell. People in hell are experiencing ultimate alienation from God in a way that's analogous to a child experiencing alienation from their parent while in time out. They're strongly experiencing, from their perspective, the absence of their parent, even though their parent may be very close. This is why hell can be described as both being cast away from God, and torment "in the presence of the holy angels and of the Lamb [Rev 14:10].") People insist on an existence without him, and so God complies, giving them what they think they want. The difference is that the Christian universalist doesn't accept the idea that God unlovingly binds the lost eternally in their state of deception and delusion. He gives them what they *think* they want in order to show them *it's not really what they want!* This isn't torture, it's punishment intended to bring clarity leading to repentance and restoration.

Anyone who's struggled with addictions, or who has worked with those bound in addiction, has seen that some people have to hit absolute rock bottom before they come to a sense of clarity about their own problem. We see something similar in the story of the prodigal son and his father (Luke 15:11–32). The father gives the son his inheritance, hardening or strengthening him in his resolve and in his ability to pursue a self-destructive path, a path that would end in a pigpen—a horrible end that brings perfect clarity to this prodigal son. The universal reconciliation and restoration view is that, for many, hell *is* the pigpen. Hell is where many will come to that place of clarity and repentance. It's the tough love of God, allowing his strong-willed, rebellious children to get exactly what they *think* they want, to show them what they *really* need and want. God will use anything—even our own rebellion—to bring the very last of his sheep back to him.

So, is this wishful thinking? Are we just making this up? What did we see when we searched the Scriptures in chapters 7 and 8? God desires to save everyone. We see this clearly in Scripture. We also see in Scripture that some people will be lost when they die and will experience hell. But we also saw passage after passage that tell us God will ultimately reconcile and restore everyone, all of his creation. And we saw in Revelation that even the evil, rebellious kings of the earth—who were cast into the lake of fire—eventually come into the city, the new Jerusalem, the heaven-on-earth church of God.[7] This is God's plan. He has bound *everyone* over to disobedience that he might have mercy on *everyone*.

The alternative is that either God doesn't love some people and desire for them to be saved, or that he's not able to save them. But we don't see either of these in Scripture. We believe that God desires and intends to save everyone he has created, and that he is well able to accomplish everything he desires and intends. We believe that our perfect God has always had a perfect end for his perfect plan. As Thomas Talbott describes, he is the grandmaster chess player who doesn't need to control our moves but who is always twelve steps ahead of us—and who is assured to win.[8] And this is a good thing for all of us!

"But no one can be saved after death!"

We encountered this claim before when we examined the eternal conscious torment view. We saw this idea is often assumed, but the Scriptures never actually say this. This assertion is often thrown out as a theological challenge to universal salvation though, so let's consider it in this context. The idea here is that physical death is final, that we must come to faith in this life before we die, and that after someone dies there's simply no way for them to be saved. But does this make sense theologically?

7. MacDonald, *Evangelical Universalist*, 114–20.
8. Talbott, *Inescapable Love*, 170.

Imagine, again, that you have a large family. And, let's say you take the whole family to visit the Grand Canyon. You give your kids a very clear warning: *"Over there, on the other side of that rock wall, is a huge canyon. If you go past that wall, you'll fall off the edge, drop for a long, long way with nothing to stop you, and you'll die!! So stay back from the edge! Don't go too close!"* One of your kids ignores your warning, climbs over the wall, and falls off the edge. But they're able to grab a rock jutting out of the canyon wall, and they're dangling there within easy reach of the top. So, you go over and stand at the edge, looking down at them, and say: *"Didn't I tell you? Didn't I say that would happen? Now there you are—past the edge! I can't do anything for you now! You're going to fall and die!"* Does that sound right to you? Is God like this parent?

Do we have *any* reason to think that after a lost person dies God no longer loves them? After they die, does God no longer have the *power* to save them? Is our human death a time limit not only for us, but for *God*? What makes us so arrogant as to assume—with no basis in Scripture—that through all of eternity God can only accomplish his will for someone in the space of one fleeting human lifetime? On whose authority do *we* confidently pronounce no one can be saved after death?

"Anyone who believes this won't be motivated to share the gospel with others."

It's very ironic to hear this challenge come from Calvinists (and we do), because this is the very same challenge *they* receive sometimes! How many times have we heard someone say: *"If God has already determined who will be saved, then there isn't any point sharing the gospel with anyone!"* Some say this to imply that people who hold this belief don't care about sharing the faith with unbelievers. Now, this isn't true of Calvinists (Calvinist believers are often some of the most passionate about evangelism, missions, and church-planting), and it's not true of evangelical universalists either. In fact, many who embrace this truth describe a striking change of perspective. It's amazing when we realize that every single person we come into contact with is someone *who will eventually come to faith in Christ*. We begin to see that *no one is a lost cause!*

Not only does this mean we can't ever mentally dismiss anyone, but it also gives us great confidence and enthusiasm in evangelism. *Everyone* with whom we share the faith will eventually repent and believe! Everyone is saveable! This doesn't make us *less* interested in evangelism, it makes us much more *eager* to share the truth and love of Christ with everyone, because we know they'll ultimately embrace this truth! We still don't know *when* this will happen for any one individual; we're still dependent on the Holy Spirit to work in their hearts and minds in his perfect time. Belief in God's ultimate, universal reconciliation and restoration makes us more eager to share the gospel, but it also makes us less strident and anxious (and—let's admit it—less obnoxious) about it. We can relax, and have a calm, confident patience about the process, knowing at some point each person will know the truth and believe. We can have an absolute, unshakable confidence that some day God will bring this person to the point where they see his light, know his love, and place their faith in Jesus Christ. Every person we encounter is someone God will make his child; each one is a future brother or sister! And so we're eager and excited to share Christ with them, as they're open (1 Pet 3:15–16), and to help them come to faith when they're ready!

"If this is true, why aren't the Scriptures more clear and explicit that all will be saved?"

This was something I wrestled with at one time, so I understand the question. Let's think about a few things. First, we do see a great many passages that clearly and explicitly tell us everyone will be reconciled to God and restored. There's actually much more clear, explicit biblical support for this belief than there is for many other beliefs we take for granted.

Also remember the Old Testament only clearly mentions resurrection once. This doesn't mean it wasn't true, just that God hadn't revealed everything to them yet. We also saw in the story of Jonah that God gave him a message of judgment, but didn't reveal how he would relent from that judgment if they repented. We can never presume to know every detail of what God's going to do. And—as with Jonah—we should assume that God is loving and merciful, eager to relent from destroying people.

"Still," some might say, "why don't the passages that speak of hell also tell us that people won't be there forever, that they will eventually be saved?" But remember, hell is the punishment of God for those who are persisting in rebellion. If you were warning your children of some impending punishment, how many of you would include the comforting detail that the punishment won't last forever? "If you disobey me you'll sit in your room without any electronic devices—*but don't worry, it won't last forever!*" We don't do that, do we? It's not that it's untrue; it's just not helpful in the moment. It actually wouldn't make sense for God to add to the passages warning of hell that they'll still be saved. We find this truth in other passages.

And there's one other possibility to consider. God shared with Abraham his plan to destroy Sodom and Gomorrah (Gen 18:16–33). Abraham responds by contending with God for them: "Will not the Judge of all the earth do right?" And we see in the passage that this is exactly what God intended. He wanted Abraham to respond this way, and encourages him to continue. Later, God tells Moses to get out of the way, that he's going to destroy the people of Israel and start over again with him. Again we see someone, this time Moses, pleading with God on behalf of the people (Exod 32:9–14). Either God had lost control and needed to be talked down by Moses, or Moses did what God wanted him to do all along. He stood in the gap for the people. He put himself on the line, pleading with God to forgive and not destroy them. And, of course, we know that Moses was foreshadowing Christ, pointing forward to the one who would perfectly stand in the gap for all people, seeking the forgiveness, reconciliation, and restoration of each person—as God always intended. We then see Paul also standing in the gap for the people, willing to put his own life on the line so his fellow Jews could be saved (Rom 9:1–3).

If God desired Abraham to have a heart for people that would cause him to appeal to God for them to be saved; if he desired Moses to put his life on the line to plead that God would show mercy to the people and relent from judgment; if we see this heart in Christ himself, in his sacrifice and in his prayer for the very people who were killing him; if we later see this same heart in Paul toward his people who were stubbornly rejecting their own Messiah—*maybe this is the heart he wants us to have toward the lost as well.* Maybe he's not as clear as he could be in Scripture in order to see if *we* will have a heart that longs for each person to be reconciled to God and restored, or if we'll have a heart that either calls for fire from heaven to destroy our enemies (Luke 9:52–55), or hearts that cause us to simply shrug our shoulders in indifference at the fate of the lost.

It doesn't surprise me at all that people would struggle with what is, for them, new and very different ideas concerning hell and who will be saved. I would actually discourage anyone from embracing too quickly any change of view. It's good for us to wrestle with these things, to question, and to challenge, and search the Scriptures for ourselves. What has surprised me, and deeply troubled me, is the *anger* I sense in many responses to this belief. Why would the thought that God might actually save everyone cause any Christian to respond with anger? Shouldn't we be moved with compassion for the lost as Christ was? Shouldn't we desire that all be saved as God does? Aren't we to love even our enemies? Why are we so often like Jonah, who was angry that God would relent from judging Nineveh, or like the older brother of the prodigal, who was angry that his father would take his lost brother back and restore him? Why are our hearts too often like these hard-hearted people in Scripture . . . *instead of like Christ's?*

If we must come to the conclusion that God won't actually save everyone, shouldn't that be a sad realization? And if we do become convinced that God not only wants to save everyone but will, wouldn't that result in tremendous rejoicing, praise, and worship? *Isn't this what we want?* And wouldn't this bring God even more glory, to be a God who doesn't have to eliminate his enemies or imprison them as they persist in rebellion, but a God who completely triumphs over every enemy by bringing them to the point of perfect clarity where they surrender to him, embrace his truth and love and grace for them, and are transformed from enemies into servants and even his children?

I believe God has always had the perfect end to his perfect plan. I believe his truth and his love are not only unconquerable, but that nothing in all creation can ultimately and finally stand against God's truth and God's love. Nothing.

PART FOUR

Closing Thoughts

Chapter Twelve

Closing Thoughts and Recommended Reading

THANK YOU FOR STICKING with me to the end of this book. It's not easy to read something that challenges what you've always believed, and even harder to fairly consider it. The fact you're still reading tells me you're like the Bereans we hear about in Scripture (Acts 17:11–12). You're not assuming the views you now hold are automatically right just because *you* hold them; you're willing to go back to the Scriptures to make sure your beliefs are truly faithful to the Word of God. Regardless of what conclusions you reach, I commend you for being willing to fairly and respectfully consider other views.

As I've mentioned throughout this book, I don't encourage anyone to change their views too quickly. Take your time; study the Scriptures prayerfully and carefully; think through the cases for the different views. What do the Scriptures actually say? Which understanding of hell is most in harmony with the biblical character of God, with the gospel of Jesus Christ, and with the broader biblical story of God's plan?

At the end of this chapter, I've listed some books I think could be helpful to you. If you're still interested after reading this, you might check out some of them. Read them prayerfully, with an open Bible, ready to verify what's written. Our commitment is above all else to biblical truth. Ultimately, the question for all of us is: What does Scripture actually teach? Or, as a question from my own church tradition asks: *"Where stands it written?"*

I've had numerous discussions with friends as we've explored these ideas. Many of us have experienced a similar process as we've worked through the case for universal reconciliation and restoration. We somehow become aware of a view we've not encountered before, and we're intrigued, but not at all convinced. After some examination, we come to acknowledge that someone can believe in universal salvation and still be a faithful, biblically-grounded evangelical—even if we still don't agree with them. But then, as we continue to read and study, we find ourselves surprisingly *unable to refute* this belief biblically or theologically. Next, we begin to realize that the *more* we study, the more we're becoming convinced from the Scriptures this view is actually true. Finally, we come to a point where we're so overwhelmed with the beauty and wonder of this scriptural truth—how much it brings glory to God and how much it's profoundly in harmony with the gospel of Christ and the biblical story—that we can't imagine it *not* being true!

It's somewhat like a page of wavy patterns we're told contains a picture of, say, a boat. At first we can't see anything, but once we see the boat— clearly and unmistakably—there's no way we can *unsee* it. Once we've seen it, it's obvious, and it's hard to understand how we never saw it before. That's what this has been like for many of us.

There may come a time in any believer's life when we have to take a similar stand to that of Martin Luther as he stood alone before the church council called to judge him. Because he was convinced his beliefs were taken directly from the Word of God, he couldn't recant these beliefs on the mere human authority of a particular church leader or council. He was open to being convinced "by the testimony of the Scriptures or by clear reason," but otherwise said he remained "bound by the Scriptures I have quoted and my conscience is captive to the Word of God." None of *us* are claiming to be another Martin Luther, of course. But we would take a very similar approach regarding our biblical conviction that God will ultimately reconcile and restore all of his creation. We're open to being convinced by Scripture and reason that we're wrong, but we can't betray our consciences and what we've seen in God's Word for the sake of any human authority.

Once again, I want to express my deep gratitude to Thomas Talbott and Robin Parry for what they've written on this subject. Everything in this book has been affected and influenced by their thinking. I'm also incredibly appreciative of the gracious and irenic spirit with which they interact with others, patiently explaining beliefs that seem strange and disconcerting to many. It's been apparent to me their desire to genuinely help and edify others and to not fall into mere polemics or confrontation. My desire has been to emulate both the clarity of their content and their winsome tone. I pray I've succeeded in doing this, and that, whatever your ultimate conclusions, this book has been helpful and edifying to you.

I've added two extra chapters for anyone who would like just a little more, but these aren't essential to understanding the basic view of universal reconciliation and restoration. The first extra chapter gives a brief answer to the question *What about Annihilationism?* The final chapter explores *Calvinism, Arminianism, and Universalism,* suggesting ways that evangelical universalism can beautifully resolve some of the nagging weaknesses many have perceived in both Calvinism and Arminianism.

For Even More Reading

If you'd like to read some books that present and compare the differing views on the nature of hell, I'd take a look at some of these:

- *Four Views on Hell* (2nd ed.) edited by Preston M. Sprinkle (Robin Parry represents evangelical universalism in his chapter and responses.)
- *All You Want to Know about Hell: Three Christian Views of God's Final Solution to the Problem of Sin* by Steve Gregg
- *Universal Salvation? The Current Debate* edited by Robin Parry and Christopher Partridge (This particularly examines the views of Thomas Talbott.)
- *Perspectives on Election: 5 Views* edited by Chad Owen Brand (Thomas Talbott represents universal reconciliation in his chapter and responses.)

For books on evangelical universalism, I would heartily recommend:

- *The Inescapable Love of God* (2nd ed.) by Thomas Talbott
- *The Evangelical Universalist* (2nd ed.) by Gregory MacDonald (This is Robin Parry writing under a pseudonym to protect the Christian publisher for whom he worked at the time.)

You can also find some very helpful videos regarding evangelical universalism featuring Robin Parry on YouTube, etc.

There are a number of other books that could be helpful to you concerning Christian universalism (and more being written), but I'd start with the ones listed above.

If you want to dig into the views of Christian leaders throughout the history of the church, I'd recommend:

- *A Larger Hope? Universal Salvation from Christian Beginnings to Julian of Norwich* by Ilaria Ramelli
- *A Larger Hope? Universal Salvation from the Reformation to the Nineteenth Century* by Robin Parry with Ilaria Ramelli
- *"All Shall Be Well" Explorations in Universalism and Christian Theology, from Origen to Moltmann* edited by Gregory MacDonald (Robin Parry)

PART FIVE

A Little Extra

Chapter Thirteen

What about Annihilationism?

You MAY HAVE NOTICED I haven't directly addressed the view of annihilationism—also known as *conditionalism*—in this book (until now). This isn't due to a lack of respect for those who hold this view, or because I don't include it as a legitimate option for sincere, faithful evangelical Christians. I certainly agree there were Christian leaders and thinkers who held this position in the early church, and it's very worthy of careful consideration and discussion for us today. I'm not able to comprehensively address the arguments for this view in one brief chapter—whole books have been written propounding this belief—but I do want to offer some general thoughts and responses.

What Is Annihilationism, Again?

Before we get into the arguments for and against this view, let's remind ourselves what it is. The annihilationist view stresses that separation from God causes death, and this death is understood to mean that the person who *dies* completely ceases to consciously exist. Annihilationists believe the consequence for ultimately rejecting God is eternal, but that no one will consciously experience an eternity of suffering. They believe hell, the second death, actually kills the lost person in the sense they no longer exist.

A Word about Terminology

Many who hold this view refer to it as "conditionalism." All who affirm the annihilationist position believe in something known as "conditional immortality." What is conditional immortality? The idea here is that human beings are not *intrinsically* immortal. God is the only one who is inherently immortal, and we can only experience immortality in him. We are only immortal *in Christ*. So, immortality—our ability to exist eternally—is only for those who are in Christ, those who receive his life, not for the lost in hell. Consequently the judgment of hell actually brings about their death in the sense that it causes them to cease to exist. They are annihilated.

There's a bit of problem, though, in distinguishing this view of hell as "conditionalism." Someone who holds one of the other views of hell—whether eternal conscious torment or universal restoration—can also believe in conditional immortality. They can believe humans aren't inherently immortal but only receive their immortality from God. Certainly this would make eternal hell more gruesome because God would then be actively sustaining the lost in eternal conscious torment, but these beliefs aren't incompatible. And there's nothing preventing a Christian universalist from believing in conditional immortality, indeed many seem to believe this very thing. So, the term *conditionalism* is perfectly in harmony with the annihilationist view—and even necessary for it—but it doesn't adequately distinguish this view from the others. This is why I continue to use the term *annihilationism* to refer to this view, because it communicates more clearly its distinguishing aspects.

Already Covered (Albeit Briefly)

You've probably noticed that I actually *have* mentioned the annihilationism view in many places throughout this book. I've often been focusing on the question "Will anyone be eternally lost?" The way we answer this question distinguishes universal salvation from both eternal conscious torment *and* annihilationism. Many of the challenges to the eternal conscious torment view also challenge annihilationism, and I've included both views in many of my comments.

We noted that love is an essential aspect of the character of God, that God can no more be unloving than he can be unholy. We can ask in what sense hell is loving, how would it be in the best interest of the lost. We can equally ask the same thing of annihilationism. Is killing people for all eternity a loving act? Is it in their best interest? How can it be what's best for them when they were created for loving relationship with God for all eternity just as we were? How can it be loving—in their best interest—to snuff them out of existence? How can heaven be truly heaven for us if our dearly loved spouses, parents, siblings, children have been annihilated, ceasing to exist forever? How can we grieve but with hope (1 Thess 4:13) if we'll never see these loved ones again? How can God claim to love me if he doesn't also love my spouse or parent or sibling or child?[1] Does God not love the lost enough to save them? Or is he unable to save them? These challenges apply to both eternal conscious torment *and* annihilationism.

If God's desire is to save everyone (1 Tim 2:4; 2 Pet 3:9), in what way is he victorious if a great many, possibly the vast majority, of his creation will never be saved? If the lost are lost to God, and he wishes to restore to himself what he has lost (Luke 15),[2] how is he victorious if he never restores to himself many or most of what he has lost? In what way has he made "everything new" (Rev 21:5)? If many or most of God's creation will remain dead for all eternity, in what way has God been victorious over death? In what sense has he destroyed his last enemy, death (1 Cor 15:26), if anyone remains dead? How is the triumphant challenge, "O death, where is your victory? O death, where is your sting?" (1 Cor 15:55) not an empty boast if death can respond: *"Right here! In the countless billions of your precious creation who I will hold in my clutches for all eternity!"*

How is God victorious if he is doing to his own creation what the *enemy* wants done to God's creation—killing and destroying them (John 10:10)? How is the universal praise and worship of God we see in passages such as Isa 45:22–24, Phil 2:9–11, and Rev 5:13 not hollow and artificial when it's only accomplished by killing all of those who refuse to praise and worship him? Isn't this like a president or prime minister boasting of unanimous support when they've silenced or eliminated anyone who would oppose them?[3] Is this truly the glorious victory of God? Is the God of the Bible truly a God who achieves universal worship by exterminating anyone who resists worshiping him—and then triumphantly exults in his "victory"?

Which view is most consistent with both the biblical character of God and with the gospel? Is the gospel really about the salvation of a few and

1. Talbott, *Inescapable Love*, 126–29.
2. Gregg, *All You Want*, 57.
3. Parry, "Universalist Response," 91.

the *annihilation* of most? Is God a God who permanently terminates his enemies,[4] or one who transforms his enemies (Rom 5:10), making peace with them and reconciling them to himself (Col 1:20), making them righteous (Rom 5:18–19), and even adopting them as his children (Rom 8:15–17)? Which one is most consistent with the entire biblical story of a creation perfectly created, ruined, and then restored?

In his response to the terminal punishment view (i.e., annihilationism), Robin Parry addresses this question:

> The problem is that God's answer to evil here is not a *gospel* solution (i.e., to eradicate sin from the sinners), but a terminator solution (i.e., to eradicate the sinners themselves). This is a drastic way of winning creation—like winning all the votes in an election by killing those who would have voted differently. Hypothetically, God could annihilate the vast majority of human beings and then claim to have won a glorious triumph in a universe filled with creatures that love him. But is this not a pyrrhic victory? The cost of winning was so very high. And given that this was a cost that God really did not want to pay, then it is as much a failure as a victory. It looks to me as if on this view sin and death have their wicked way in the end—forcing God to abandon and obliterate many of those he loves.[5]

Over-Interpreting Key Words

This view relies to a great degree on particular understandings of certain words in Scripture, what many of us would see as over-interpretation of these words. This is a bit ironic because we determined the eternal conscious torment view to also rest essentially on the misinterpretation of one word. Just as—once we understand the meaning of aionios—we see no place where Scripture describes eternal conscious torment, so we find no passage of Scripture that clearly and unambiguously describes the lost as ceasing to exist. But we do hear many proponents of this view emphasizing certain key words. So, let's briefly look at some of these words.

It's common for annihilationists to summarize their belief by calling our focus to all the places in Scripture that describe the ultimate fate of the lost as death (such as Rom 6:23), and then stressing: *dead means dead. It*

---

4. Parry, "Universalist Response," 89–92.
5. Parry, "Universalist Response," 91; emphasis in original.

doesn't make any sense, we're told, *for "death" to mean anything other than actual death, as in ceasing to exist.* And this sounds simple and compelling, honoring the wording of Scripture. The problem is the Bible often uses the word death in ways that obviously don't mean annihilation.

Let's look at one example in Eph 2:1–5:

> As for you, you were dead in your transgressions and sins, in which you used to live when you followed the ways of this world and of the ruler of the kingdom of the air, the spirit who is now at work in those who are now disobedient. All of us also lived among them at one time, gratifying the cravings of our flesh and following its desires and thoughts. Like the rest, we were by nature deserving of wrath. But because of his great love for us, God, who is rich in mercy, made us alive with Christ even when we were dead in transgressions—it is by grace you have been saved.

We see here that we were previously *living* in a state of *death—existing* but needing to be *made alive*. This is common language in the Bible, a common way to speak of death. So, it's not at all nonsensical to speak of people "existing in a state of death" when we speak of the judgment of hell. Some will go so far as to argue that death in the Bible primarily (or often) explicitly means a total cessation of existence. I can't find even one place in Scripture where the word death unambiguously connotes such an idea. Since death can be used in very different ways—often meaning to exist in a state of death spiritually, and other times meaning simply the end of one's physical life—to argue that "dead means dead *in the sense of ceasing to exist*" is circular reasoning, assuming one's point to make one's point.

Some argue that the Greek word translated "perish" in verses such as John 3:16 (*apollumi*) actually means to die in the sense of ceasing to exist. In the New Testament, this Greek word most often means "to be lost." For instance the familiar parables we read in Luke 15 that speak of the sheep, the coin, and the prodigal son that are "lost," all use this same Greek word we find in John 3:16. This is why at least three translations render John 3:16 as should "not be lost but have eternal life" (ISV, NCV, and Phillips). Of course, being lost doesn't necessitate being annihilated.

But this word also frequently conveys the meanings of to perish, or to be ruined, or destroyed. So, let's think about the word "perish." What does it mean for something to perish? When we say something is "perishable," what do we mean? If you leave something that's perishable indefinitely in your refrigerator, does it cease to exist? We'd probably wish it *would* cease to exist! What does it do? It decays, it rots. It might even decay to the point we no longer know what it is! But it doesn't cease to exist. It actually continues to exist but in a *ruined state*.

It's surprising to me how many of those who hold this view refer to the ruined wineskin Jesus spoke of in Matt 9:17 to support the idea of annihilation. The point often made is that the ruined wineskin would have to be discarded. The problem is that the *text* doesn't say anything about discarding the wineskin. The ruined wineskin doesn't cease to exist; it continues in a state of ruin. Now, someone could subsequently discard the ruined wineskin, but they also may not. To discard the wineskin would be a separate act. The fact that the wineskin is ruined does not mean or require that it ceases to exist. (Actually, even if it's discarded, it doesn't cease to exist.)

We have the same problem with the word "destroy." This sounds very extreme, no doubt, but it doesn't require a cessation of existence. One can easily think of a car, a building, or a city that is destroyed but continues to exist in a ruined state. We even refer to a destroyed city or building as "ruins." And we also can't forget the extensive pattern we saw in Scripture that what God destroys he also restores.

It's often emphasized that fire consumes things. And it can certainly do this, that's true. But we all know that Scripture also speaks of fire as something that *purifies* instead of destroying. Actually fire often destroys *and* purifies at the same time, burning away the dross and leaving the purified silver or gold. We can't simply assume a particular connotation for fire. Fire does consume, but it doesn't *only* consume, and it doesn't *always* consume.

My point here is there is no lexical or textual basis for claiming that the words "death," "destroy," "perish," "ruin," or "fire" in Scripture require or even suggest that anyone ceases to consciously exist, or that they're ruined or destroyed beyond hope of restoration. It would be inappropriate to assume this meaning, and then use this assumed meaning as a basis on which to establish this belief. This is going beyond the meaning of the text and reading into it something that's not explicitly and unambiguously there already.

Theological Inconsistencies

Many annihilationists rightly stress that they, too, believe in God's judgment of the lost in hell. They point out that their belief includes the suffering of unrepentant sinners in hell, in a way that corresponds to the individual's sins. They're clear that the unsaved will suffer to a greater or lesser extent depending on their actual sins. In a chapter on "terminal punishment" (i.e., annihilationism), John Stackhouse Jr. explains repeatedly that the unsaved must suffer in hell in order to "make their own atonement" for their sins.[6]

But, wait a minute . . . hasn't Jesus already atoned for the sins of the whole world (1 John 2:2; John 1:29)?[7] One might respond, *"Yes, but if people don't accept Christ's atonement for them, they must atone for their own sins."* Fair enough. So—since they have rejected the atonement of Christ (or if Christ never intended to atone for their sins)—they must atone for their own sins. And according to annihilationists such as Stackhouse, the lost do this by suffering in hell.

But this begs an important question: If the lost reach a point in their suffering when they have somehow atoned for their own sins, *why are they then annihilated?* If they've actually atoned for their own sins—atoning for their sin that separated them from God—why are they not restored to God? Isn't this the very essence of the word atonement, intentionally combining the words at-one-ment? If they've atoned for their own sins, why are they not then at one with God as the word requires? This seems to me confusingly inconsistent theologically.

(Please understand, Christian universalists aren't arguing that the lost actually *do* atone for their sins by suffering in hell. I'm simply responding to an annihilationist argument, and showing where I think it's theologically problematic.)

Some annihilationists don't believe people will atone for their sins by suffering in hell. Some believe hell is simply the means of execution for the lost; it's the way God brings their life to an end. They are cast into hell and they die because, we're reminded, humans are not intrinsically immortal. If we don't have eternal life in Christ, then we will naturally die in hell and cease to exist.

But this brings up even more questions. If "dead is dead," what is the state of the lost when they die in this lifetime? Do they cease to exist? How could they not, since the human soul is not immortal? Or is the soul not immortal . . . but it's a *bit* more immortal than the body? Does the soul have a slightly longer shelf-life? Is God supernaturally *sustaining* the souls of the

---

6. Stackhouse, "Terminal Punishment," 61–79.

7. Yes, I do understand many Calvinists wouldn't agree that Christ atoned for the sins of the world, although this seems to directly contradict the Scriptures I referenced.

lost . . . until he annihilates them? Or does the lost person actually cease to exist when they die now, and then when God resurrects the lost (Dan 12:2; Rev 20:11–13), he's actually *re-creating* them? But then why would God re-create someone who had ceased to exist . . . just to painfully exterminate them again? That seems pretty chilling! But if the soul does live on beyond the body . . . just how much fire does it take to consume a soul?

The more we actually think this through, the more confusing and theologically problematic it becomes. It might sound as if I'm being overly technical and unfairly nitpicky in demanding this kind of clarity about death. But remember, it's the annihilationism view that insists "dead means dead," and that this *must* mean ceasing to consciously exist. If we're being asked to accept this kind of definition as absolute—and even use it as a foundational basis for this view—I don't think it's too much to ask for it to consistently make sense. I just don't see how it does.

The Strong Case for Universal Reconciliation and Restoration

When annihilationism was beginning to be considered again and discussed back in the 1980s and '90s, few were including Christian universalism in the broader discussion. What's interesting is that when we go back and read the cases for annihilationism at that time, they were using many of the passages and challenges to eternal conscious torment that evangelical universalists use now. This makes us ask: *Doesn't universal reconciliation and restoration fit these passages even better? Doesn't it challenge eternal conscious torment even more effectively? And isn't annihilationism actually vulnerable to many of the same challenges?*

For example, Clark Pinnock challenged eternal conscious torment by writing,

> What purpose of God would be served by the unending torture of the wicked except sheer vengeance and vindictiveness? Such a fate would spell endless and totally unredemptive suffering, punishment just for its own sake. But unending torment would be the kind of utterly pointless and wasted suffering which could never lead to anything good beyond it.[8]

And John Wenham agrees:

---

8. Pinnock, cited by Gregg, *All You Want to Know*, 210.

> Whatever anyone says, unending torture speaks to me of sadism, not justice.[9]

But couldn't the same challenges be made of annihilationism? Don't these statements from Pinnock and Wenham actually challenge any punishment that is purely retributive (that is, based solely on punishment rather than also the rehabilitation of the offender), punishment for punishment's sake, any punishment that isn't loving and redemptive?

What if we use the same quotes above, but replace the words "endless" and "unending" with "purely retributive" punishment "followed by complete annihilation"? Let's try it:

> What purpose of God would be served by the purely retributive torture of the wicked followed by complete annihilation expect sheer vengeance and vindictiveness? Such a fate would spell purely retributive and totally unredemptive suffering, punishment just for its own sake. But purely retributive torment followed by complete annihilation would be the kind of utterly pointless and wasted suffering which could never lead to anything good beyond it.

> Whatever anyone says, purely retributive torment followed by complete annihilation speaks to me of sadism, not justice.

Don't these challenges apply just as well to annihilationism? We can find many arguments for annihilationism that present it as somehow merciful. But the absolute extermination of human beings, causing them to completely cease to exist, can only be considered merciful when compared to the horror of endless, hopeless torment. When we add biblical universalism to the discussion, annihilation doesn't seem so merciful anymore. It's only slightly less horrific than the traditional view.

In more recent works, we similarly see proponents of this view not taking the Scriptures quite far enough. In *Four Views on Hell*, John Stackhouse Jr. ends his response to eternal conscious torment[10] by quoting Ps 30:5 from the NRSV:

> For his anger is but for a moment;
> his favor is for a lifetime.
> Weeping may linger for the night,
> but joy comes with the morning.

---

9. Wenham, quoted by Gregg, *All You Want to Know*, 210.
10. Stackhouse, "Terminal Punishment Response," 47.

But you can see how we might read this and think, *"Doesn't this passage fit biblical universalism even better?"* If God is—in his wrath—permanently and eternally annihilating people, causing them to cease to exist, how is his anger only lasting for a moment? The effects of his anger will certainly continue for all eternity. And, from the annihilationist view, is the weeping during the night truly replaced by *joy* in the morning? Isn't this torment replaced by extermination? That may provide a kind of relief, in some sense, to a person being tormented—but could we, with a straight face, call this *joy*? When someone is on death row and their final appeal is denied, is that the time they rejoice? Would joy come with their execution, especially if there was absolutely no hope for anything past this death, only completely ceasing to exist for all eternity? Even compared to eternal conscious torment, this is still horrific, just a little less intolerable.

When we include Christian universalism in the discussion, the reference to these kinds of passages from annihilationists seems more than a little ironic. In a similar way, the frequent references of annihilationists to the utter destruction of Sodom don't have the desired impact on evangelical universalists. This isn't only because the destruction of Sodom wasn't the same as cessation of existence, but because God tells us explicitly in Scripture he will *restore* the Sodom he utterly destroyed (Ezek 16:46–63)!

Because for most of us eternal conscious torment has been, by far, the dominant view, many annihilationists and conditionalists have welcomed evangelical universalists somewhat as allies. This makes sense, and I certainly appreciate it, and am perfectly willing to reciprocate when appropriate. I have deep respect and admiration for a great many annihilationist leaders and scholars. But as Christian universalism has been increasingly discussed and its influence has been growing, I've heard from an annihilationist friend a certain amount of frustration that relatively few (from his perspective) are considering conditionalism but seem to be leapfrogging immediately to the universal restoration view. He wanted to know, "Why is that?"

The process of reexamining my views of hell and the bases for the view I once held reminds me a great deal of a much earlier process I went through of reexamining my view of the rapture of the church and the bases for it. I grew up in churches that held to what is known as "classic dispensationalism." For those who are unfamiliar with this term, a distinguishing aspect of classic dispensationalism is the understanding the return of Christ will be preceded by seven years of tribulation, with the rapture of the church usually occurring prior to this period of tribulation. Many would refer to this as the "Left Behind" view of the end times. Because this view emphasizes the rapture happening *before* the tribulation, it's commonly known as the "pretribulation" view, or "pretrib" for short.

My early ministry was very much in a classic dispensational, pretrib context. But at a certain point, I was driven to reexamine and reevaluate my beliefs about the rapture. This caused me to carefully study the core beliefs supporting what I had been taught. When I examined the foundational claims of my classic dispensational view of a pretribulational rapture, I found them insupportable. When, much later, I examined the foundational claims for eternal conscious torment, I reached a very similar conclusion.

But there's another interesting similarity here. When I first decided to reexamine my views of the rapture, it seemed I had to weigh through a large number of possible views: pretrib, midtrib, posttrib, pre-wrath, etc. But I quickly realized the primary question I had to answer was: *Does the Bible present the rapture and the return of Christ as separate events or as aspects of the same event?* When I looked at it this way, the choice for me was between historic premillennialism (the view of the early church that the rapture is part of the same event as Christ's return to earth) and all the other views. I had known about the midtribulational view, of course. I personally knew a few people who held this view. They tended to be very intelligent students of Scripture, and they had their arguments focusing on what they thought to be key details in Scripture. But I quickly came to see this view as a variation on a theme, an adjustment of the classic pretrib view.

When I eventually came to reject the classic dispensational view in which I had been brought up, I went right to historic premillennialism. Others leaving classic dispensationalism have moved to an amillennial view. But I don't know anyone who's moved away from classic dispensationalism to the midtrib view. That's because it's simply a variation on the same theme, it's a modification of the classic pretrib view. Now, even if you completely disagree with my conclusions about the rapture, hopefully you can understand the thought process I'm describing. And I think you can see where I'm going with this.

When I decided to reexamine what I believed about hell and why, it seemed I would need to sort through extensive arguments for all the different views. (And I did read a fair amount from annihilationist scholars.) But I quickly began to focus on one key question: *Does the Bible teach that anyone will be eternally lost?* In much the same way as before, when we look at the issue in this light, it distinguishes biblical universalism from all other views. Annihilationism answers this question in the same way eternal conscious torment does. It's still a variation on the same theme.

Ultimately the answer to the question I and others have received: *Why aren't you more seriously considering anniliationism?* is that I'm already thoroughly convinced God does love everyone and intends for everyone to be reconciled to him and completely restored, that he is more than able to accomplish everything he intends, and that he has planned for all of this from the very beginning, that this very outcome was woven all through his creation from the start. I don't see any clear passages of Scripture explicitly telling us the lost will suffer eternal conscious torment *or* that they will ultimately be annihilated. But I do see in Scripture that nothing is lost or destroyed or ruined beyond God's ability to heal and restore, and that he restores everything he judges and destroys. I find a great many passages clearly and explicitly telling us that God will reconcile and restore *all* of his creation, that *everyone* will come to him and worship him.

I find the theological arguments for both eternal conscious torment and annihilationism to be problematic and unconvincing (often in the very same ways). But the more I study the Scriptures and the more I consider these things in a more broadly theological way, the more I'm convinced that, *of course God will save all of those he has created!* Does God still love the lost? Of course, he does. Is God still able to save them? Of course, he is. Then why would God settle for eternally annihilating those whom he can reconcile and restore? And I contend this is exactly what we find in Scripture.

Chapter Fourteen

Calvinism, Arminianism, and Universalism

THE DEBATES BETWEEN (WHAT we now call) Calvinists and Arminians have been around for a long time, going back at least to the time of Augustine. This is an area of theology that has always fascinated me. A few years ago, Kevin DeYoung and Ted Kluck wrote a book on a completely different subject, which they titled *Why We're Not Emergent: By Two Guys Who Should Be*. They described the way much of what drew people to the emerging church at that time held a certain appeal to them as well, how they would seem like a natural fit for this movement, but why they just couldn't be part of the emerging church. I've jokingly suggested to friends I might write a similar book: *Why I'm Not a Calvinist: By a Guy Who Should Be* for much the same reasons. I appreciate the draw to Reformed theology, how much it's focused on in-depth study of Scripture, how much it seeks to glorify God above all else, how logically coherent and consistent and rich it is theologically, etc. To those who know me, I would seem like a natural fit. But—and I know this drives my Calvinist friends crazy—the *more* I study the Scriptures the more I *don't* see Calvinism there.

Whenever I study different views on a particular subject, I always want to know *why* people hold these views. I try to determine what are the core issues or concerns that are key to those advocating a certain position. Many times, a superficial perception of what's most important to differing groups isn't really accurate. For instance, many people assume that what's most important to Calvinists is that God is sovereign—that he is in control of, or determines, everything. But it doesn't take long to see that what impels most Calvinists is a profound concern for the glory of God. On the other side, many assume that what most motivates Arminians is preserving the absolute free will of the individual. But if you read much at all about why Arminians reject Calvinism, it becomes clear their chief concern is that Calvinism is inconsistent with the biblical character of God, especially his love and grace. In other words, they feel that Calvinism diminishes *the glory of God*. Ironically, both sides are motivated by very similar concerns.

Over the years, a few people have tried to ferret out some kind of mediating position that could bring Calvinists and Arminians together. And people in both camps *have* developed significant variations within both Calvinism and non-Calvinism. But the core issues related to both views have seemed to remain stubbornly unbridgeable. There just is no "Calminian" median position between the two views. Calvinists and Arminians can enjoy the fellowship and unity they share in Christ, and be completely committed to the gospel of Jesus Christ. But any attempted integration or synthesis of their distinctive views regarding election, divine providence, and human freedom have proved unworkable. So, it was very compelling to me when I began to see ways that Christian universalism shared strengths from either side of this debate while also avoiding their distinctive weaknesses. Let me give some examples.

Sovereignty and Free Will

Anyone who's followed these issues must inevitably sort through concepts such as divine sovereignty and human free will. Does God really determine everything that occurs, even our thoughts and decisions? Or are people truly free to make their own choices without being controlled in any way by an outside force? As many of us know from experience, these discussions can degenerate into endless arguments about whether or not this kind of "libertarian free will" even exists.

There are legitimate challenges to both sides, far more than we can cover in one brief chapter. We see countless examples in the Bible of God putting choices before people, and then holding them responsible for their choice. Were these choices actually free, or was their choice pre-determined by God? If God had already determined what they would choose, this would seem to make the choice God *seems* to give these people actually some kind of artificial facade. But does God really allow *so much* to ride on the decisions of his creation? Does God really allow humans to determine so much of the outcome of everything, and then simply impose on them the consequences of their choices? Isn't that a picture of a fairly passive God?

Many, possibly most, Calvinists today clarify their beliefs regarding sovereignty and free will utilizing a concept called *compatibilism*. According to this view, divine sovereignty or providence—the idea that God determines everything, even our decisions—is compatible to some extent with human choice. How is that so? It's compatible, they claim, because God can work through other factors in our lives to bring us to the point we make the choices he intends us to make. Let's say, for example, God wanted someone to choose chocolate ice cream rather than vanilla or strawberry (because, of course, chocolate is best!). Instead of simply overriding their choice and forcing them to choose chocolate, he could work through various other factors in their life to bring them to the point they would voluntarily choose chocolate. Their choice of chocolate would be freely made in the sense they were choosing what they wanted at the time, but the *desire* for chocolate would be something God intentionally brought about in the heart of the individual. So, God would be determining their choice, but—in the moment—they would be *freely* choosing what God *intended* them to choose. This is compatibilism.

Some Arminians will immediately reject this idea because it feels coercive to them, as if God is violating our free will. But wait a minute. Isn't this just a description of good parenting? I don't think many children naturally prefer vegetables and fruit to cake or candy! But what do parents do? They train their children to get them to the point they make healthy choices rather than follow their childish instincts. A good parent does this in every area of their child's life. Is this violating the child's free will? Maybe, at first it is. But the goal is for the child to *freely* make healthy choices. And this is being done for the long-term good of the child.

The problem with the Calvinist understanding of compatibilism isn't that God is determining what someone will choose, or that he may even be overriding in some sense the free will of an individual. After all, we see many examples in Scripture where God does just that. God had no problem in acting coercively when confronting King Saul in the Old Testament (1 Sam 19:23–24) and Saul of Tarsus in the New (Acts 9:1–19). We looked at this previously in chapter 11. And we must acknowledge there is much in our lives over which we have no control whatsoever (where and when we're born, to whom we're born, etc.).

No, the issue with Calvinism isn't that God works within us to bring us to the point we choose what is good, beneficial, and God-honoring rather than what is evil, destructive, and God-defying. The problem is that—according to Calvinism—he could easily do this for *everyone*, but he doesn't. So—through no choice of their own—an individual is born into a fallen human race, subjected to a rebellious sin nature before they themselves have done anything good or bad. As the apostle Paul said, "God has bound everyone over to disobedience" (Rom 11:32). God—due only to his love and grace—wonderfully rescues people from their bondage to sin and deception, and trains their hearts to choose what is good and right. *But*—according to Calvinism—while he could do this for every one of his creation, he doesn't. He leaves some hopelessly bound in sin, deception, and death with no opportunity to be saved. This is what causes the Arminian to recoil from Calvinism.

Universal reconciliation and restoration can emphasize the same free choices we see all through Scripture. But it doesn't have to be tied to the idea God won't actively influence and even, in some sense, determine our free choices for our ultimate good. Evangelical universalists can embrace the idea of a compatabilist process where God works in our wills to conform them to his—as long as God ultimately does this for everyone. Calvinists often speak of how God works through secondary causes to bring about his will in the human heart. Christian universalists would agree, and include hell as one of his secondary causes that will work his will in the hearts of those he intends to save. Is this just sentimentalism or wishful thinking? No, this is based squarely on what we saw clearly taught in Scripture, and what has been believed by many Christians throughout the history of the church.

Three Points

If you're reading this chapter, you're likely already familiar with the TULIP acronym, listing the five points of Calvinism:

T—total depravity

U—unconditional election

L—limited atonement

I—irresistible grace

P—perseverance of the saints

There is no necessary, core argument between Calvinists and Arminians regarding "total depravity" and "perseverance of the saints" (the first and fifth points), although Calvinists and non-Calvinists would certainly nuance these beliefs differently and see differing implications. It might be safest to say their understandings of these two points somewhat overlap. Regardless, because these points aren't necessary to our discussion, we're not going to spend time going over them in this chapter. The debate between Calvinists and non-Calvinists is mostly focused on the three center points. So, let's consider each of these in turn.

Unconditional Election

The U in TULIP stands for *unconditional election*. This has to do with God's "election" or choice of those who would be saved. They are, therefore, the "elect" or the chosen. Calvinists believe God's election or choice of these people has absolutely nothing to do with any prior condition God observed in the life of particular individuals, so his election is *unconditional*. Many prefer to describe this belief as *sovereign election*, emphasizing that any cause for God's choice lies only in the good pleasure of his will (drawing from Eph 1:5), not in anything inherent in lost humans.

Arminians have often countered with belief in *conditional election*, the idea that God's choice is conditioned on his foreknowing who will place their faith in Christ and who will not. Those who will believe, God chooses to save. But the Calvinist can point out an obvious weakness in this understanding: Does God simply choose those who he knows will *choose him*? Is God really that passive in this process of election or choosing, with everything riding on the choice of the individual?

Other Arminians and non-Calvinists present instead a concept of *corporate election*.[1] This view understands God's election or choice to be primarily about choosing a people, a corporate group. God has chosen to save a group from his creation and make them his church, and anyone who places their faith in Christ is saved and becomes part of this chosen people. Calvinists don't deny that God chooses to save a corporate people, but they would challenge just which one is primary: God's choice of a corporate people, or his selection of individual people whom he will save. Does God

---

1. Klein, *New Chosen People*.

choose each individual he will save, and then these individuals collectively make up his chosen people, the church? Or does he choose to save some indeterminate group, and allow individuals to self-select whether or not they will be part of the chosen people? You can see how this can quickly become a *chicken-or-the-egg* kind of debate.

Biblical universalists don't have to try to thread this needle. They don't have to prioritize either corporate election or personal election. Christian universalists will have differing nuances in their exact understanding of God's process of election or choosing. But there's nothing preventing someone who believes in universal reconciliation and restoration from affirming both that God has chosen to save a corporate people, and that he sovereignly chooses each person whom he will save and make part of his church. They just believe God has sovereignly chosen to save *each individual* he created. They believe this because that's what they see in Scripture, and because this best fits the biblical character of God. So, evangelical universalists have no problem believing that God's election is corporate, personal, unconditional, and sovereign.

Limited Atonement

This point of Calvinism is based on the understanding that Christ's sacrifice on the cross doesn't just *potentially* save people, it actually saves them. The word often used to describe Christ's atonement for us is that it was "efficacious," meaning it accomplished exactly what God intended it to accomplish. Calvinists can present an impressive biblical argument that Christ's atonement does indeed save us. Because they prefer to emphasize what God is intending to do—and actually doing—in the act of atonement, Calvinists sometimes prefer to describe this belief as *particular redemption* or *definite atonement*. But they're quite clear about the implications of this belief: everyone Christ died for is saved; only the elect will be saved; therefore, Christ died only for the elect, only for those God has already chosen to save. This is why the traditional name for this belief is *limited atonement*; the atonement is limited—in this understanding—to the elect, to those God has chosen to save.

Non-Calvinists are quick to point out some serious weaknesses in this belief, however. The conclusion that Christ died only for a select group, and not for everyone, may seem perfectly logical and even unavoidable to Calvinists, but we never see it articulated in Scripture at all. That seems strange. Not only that, but this belief seems to directly contradict passages in Scripture that say Jesus *did* in fact die as the atonement for all. Here are just a few examples:

> The next day John saw Jesus coming toward him and said, "Look, the Lamb of God, who takes away the sin of the world!" (John 1:29)

> That is why we labor and strive, because we have put our hope in the living God, who is the Savior of all people, and especially of those who believe. (1 Tim 4:10)

> He is the atoning sacrifice for our sins, and not only for ours but also for the sins of the whole world. (1 John 2:2)

There are many, many other passages we could list as well, from a wide range of Scripture.

Because this belief seems to *so* fly in the face of clear scriptural evidence to the contrary, many Calvinists have rejected this point, and refer to themselves as "four-point Calvinists." But more consistent, five-point Calvinists have an effective challenge for their four-point brothers and sisters: *Why would Christ die for those he never intended to save? What conceivable purpose would he have in doing this?* And for anyone rejecting this belief, they can ask: *So, does the atonement of Christ not actually accomplish what it's intended to accomplish?* Does it just *potentially* save people and not *actually* save them? Calvinists can argue that *this* is actually limiting the atonement of Christ! Both sides can effectively challenge each other as to whether their views are consistently sound biblically and theologically. It's hard to find *all* of the elements of either position in Scripture.

So, how do we square this circle? Amazingly, this presents no conundrum at all for the universal restorationist. We don't have to dance around what we see clearly in Scripture, or somehow introduce ideas we *don't* find there. We can simply believe *everything* we see Scripture teaching about this, and follow the Word of God where it leads us: yes, God does desire to save everyone; yes, Christ's atonement does actually save those for whom he died; yes, Christ did die for everyone and make atonement for the whole world; so, yes—as we see in Scripture—God will reconcile and restore everyone he has created. Christian universalists actually do believe Christ died specifically for the elect—we just believe that ultimately we're *all* the elect, he chose to save everyone! So, his atonement is particular, definite, and completely unlimited! Once again, we can embrace the strengths of both sides of this debate without being bound to the weaknesses of either Calvinism or Arminianism.

Irresistible Grace

It's not uncommon for non-Calvinists to mistakenly describe this belief as God *forcing* people to place their faith in him. Many Calvinists counter this challenge by explaining that once the Holy Spirit has drawn a person to Christ, once God has brought them to life, once he has freed them from deception and bondage to sin, then it's not that God doesn't *allow* them to resist, but that no one so truly freed *would* resist his love and grace. To this the evangelical universalist would say, "Amen!"

The Calvinist can question the Arminian: If God is truly providing the sinner with enough freedom and spiritual illumination for them to understand their need for salvation in Christ and the precious life in him God is offering—*how could they ever freely reject God's grace?* The Arminian has to believe people *can* freely reject God's salvation in this way because they assume not everyone will be saved (and God won't condemn people without offering a chance for them to believe). The Calvinist has to believe God bestows his grace only on a select number because of the same assumption. Those who believe in universal reconciliation and restoration reject this assumption that some of God's created humanity won't be saved—because we don't find it biblically or theologically sound—and so find no intractable problem here, either. God's grace truly is irresistible, he bestows his grace on everyone, and ultimately no one will resist. God's love and his grace will conquer all. No matter how great the sin, God's grace *always* surpasses it (Rom 5:20).

You may recall our three options from chapter 10. Do you believe in a God who *can* save everyone, but *won't*? A God who *desires* to save everyone, but *can't*? Or a God who *wants* to save everyone, *can* save everyone, so *does* save everyone? Is our choice really between a God who doesn't truly love everyone or a God who lacks the power and wisdom to ensure his loving intent isn't frustrated?

Many years ago, J. I. Packer famously summarized Calvinism with the words: "God saves sinners."[2] While Arminians will obviously take exception to this—because they too believe God saves sinners—we can understand

2. Packer, "Introductory Essay," 4–5.

how Packer intended this as a summary of the five points of Calvinism. But the universal restorationist can use the same words in a very similar way. This simple sentence beautifully summarizes Christian universalism, as well. We believe that *God saves sinners*. In fact, we believe God saves *all* sinners, and that this is wonderfully to his eternal glory. Amazingly, the perennial debates between Calvinists and Arminians are ones we can happily skip—because we can draw from the best strengths of both views!

In his letter to the Romans, Paul powerfully describes the human condition, and our need—whether Jew or gentile—for salvation. He explains clearly why we can't earn our own salvation—whether Jew or gentile—and must be saved by God's grace, justified by faith. He then explores the wonderful benefits of God's salvation, building to a crescendo in the eighth chapter. There is no longer any condemnation for us, we've been adopted as God's children, he works everything out for the good of those who love him, and nothing can separate us from his love. But this left a nagging question: *What about most of the Jews? What about most of the covenant people of God who had not come to faith in Christ?*

So, Paul begins to address this problem in chapter 9. He uses very relevant examples to show that God uses each of us in his plan according to his sovereign will, and that none of us can call him to task for how he does that. If he even hardens people (as John's Gospel speaks of the Jewish people of Jesus' day being hardened [John 12:39–40]), then it's his sovereign choice whom he hardens and to whom he shows mercy.

Then we come to vv. 22–24, where Paul speaks of objects of wrath and objects of mercy. I must first say (with much respect and affection) that I'm surprised how many wonderful, Calvinist exegetes of Scripture base so much theology on two *rhetorical questions* in Rom 9! Surely we know better than to mistake Paul's rhetorical questions for conclusions!

It also amazes me how so many assume these two questions must be referring to completely different groups of people, with all of us categorized as *either* an object of wrath *or* an object of mercy. This despite passages such as Eph 2:3–5 that tells us:

> All of us also lived among them at one time, gratifying the cravings
> of our flesh and following its desires and thoughts. Like the rest,
> we were *by nature deserving of wrath*. But because of his great love
> for us, God, *who is rich in mercy*, made us alive with Christ even
> when we were dead in transgressions—it is by grace you have been
> saved [emphasis added].

This compares well with the first three chapters of Romans that show we all share in the same sinful condition, the same condemnation, and are subject to the same divine wrath. So—for at least the elect—we *were* objects of God's wrath but have *become* objects of God's mercy. Couldn't this be true of us all? Well, it's poor biblical interpretation to look for answers in Rom 9 because this is where Paul is asking provocative *questions*. For answers we must go to chapter 11 where Paul himself explains his conclusions.

Paul begins chapter 11 by asking "Did God reject his people?" His answer? "By no means!" He then goes on to make very clear he's speaking of ethnic Israel. Had God hardened many of the Jewish people, causing them to stumble? Yes, Paul explains, that's true. But then he also clarifies in v. 11:

> Did they stumble so as to fall beyond recovery? Not at all! Rather, because of their transgression, salvation has come to the Gentiles to make Israel envious.

So, God had a sovereign purpose in the hardening of Israel. Just as he illustrated in chapter 9, he used these Jewish people in his plan according to his will. But their eventual inclusion was *also* always part of the plan.

See how he continues in v. 12:

> But if their transgression means riches for the world, and their loss means riches for the Gentiles, how much greater riches will their full inclusion bring!

He then makes clear, once again, that he's speaking of unbelieving, ethnic Israel. He uses the now well-known illustration of the domesticated olive tree (the covenant nation of Israel), the olive branches that were separated from the tree because of unbelief (the Jews that were hardened), and wild olive branches that were grafted into the tree (believing gentiles). In v. 23— still using this illustration, still speaking of unbelieving, ethnic Israel—he insists:

> And if they do not persist in unbelief, they will be grafted in, for God is able to graft them in again.

And then in vv. 25–26, in the same context, still speaking of ethnic Israel, he goes even further:

> Israel has experienced a hardening in part until the full number of the Gentiles has come in, and in this way all Israel will be saved.

So, the hardening of some of the Jewish people was always intended to be temporary, it always had a sovereign purpose in the plan of God, and it was always intended to result in "*all Israel*" being saved, including the very Israel that had experienced God's hardening. (Compare this with Isa 45:25.) It's interesting to see to what lengths people will go to try to find a way to make "all Israel" not actually mean "all Israel!" (And we won't take the time to explore what it means for "the full number of the Gentiles" to come in!)

As Paul has consistently done previously all through Romans, he shows how God is working the same in both Jews and gentiles. What is Paul's ultimate answer to the questions he's been addressing for three chapters—not only for lost, hardened Israel but for all of us? We find his conclusion in v. 32:

> For God has bound *everyone* over to disobedience so that he may
> have mercy on *them all* [emphasis added].

Reading Rom 9:22–24 in light of the first chapters of Romans and of Paul's own conclusion in 11:32, I find only one possible interpretation: God has made *everyone* objects of wrath so that he may make *us all* objects of mercy.

And just as was true of Paul, I'm not only confident of this biblical truth and hope, it fills me with *overwhelming praise and worship* for our glorious God who—alone—could accomplish this perfect outcome for all his creation! Because of this surpassingly, gloriously perfect ending to God's perfect plan, I'm driven to the same kind of worship as the apostle Paul in Rom 11, and I can think of no better words to end this book:

> *Oh, the depth of the riches of the wisdom and knowledge of God!*
> *How unsearchable his judgments,*
> *and his paths beyond tracing out!*
> *Who has known the mind of the Lord?*
> *Or who has been his counselor?*
> *Who has ever given to God,*
> *that God should repay them?*
> *For from him and through him and for him are all things.*
> *To him be the glory forever! Amen.*

Bibliography

Beale, G. K. *New International Greek Testament Commentary: The Book of Revelation.* Grand Rapids: Eerdmans, 1999.

Bruce, F. F. "Age." In *The International Standard Bible Encyclopedia*, edited by Geoffrey W. Bromiley, 1–67. Grand Rapids: Eerdmans, 1988.

———. *The Gospel of John.* Grand Rapids: Eerdmans, 1983.

Burk, Denny. "Eternal Conscious Torment." In *Four Views on Hell*, edited by Preston M. Sprinkle, 17–43. 2nd ed. Grand Rapids: Zondervan, 2016.

———. "An Eternal Conscious Torment Response." In *Four Views on Hell*, edited by Preston M. Sprinkle, 128–33. 2nd ed. Grand Rapids: Zondervan, 2016.

Carson, D. A. *Exegetical Fallacies.* 2nd ed. Grand Rapids: Baker Academic, 1996.

DeYoung, Kevin, and Ted Kluck. *Why We're Not Emergent: By Two Guys Who Should Be.* Chicago: Moody, 2008.

Evangelical Free Church of America. *Evangelical Convictions: A Theological Exposition of the Statement of Faith of the Evangelical Free Church of America.* Minneapolis: Free Church, 2011.

Garland, David E. *Luke.* Zondervan Exegetical Commentary on the New Testament 3. Grand Rapids: Zondervan, 2011.

Gregg, Steve. *All You Want to Know about Hell: Three Christian Views of God's Final Solution to the Problem of Sin.* Nashville: Thomas Nelson, 2013.

Harris, R. Laird, et al., eds. *Theological Wordbook of the Old Testament.* Chicago: Moody Bible Institute, 1980.

Jersak, Bradley. *Her Gates Will Never Be Shut.* Eugene, OR: Wipf & Stock, 2009.

Keener, Craig S. *The IVP Bible Background Commentary: New Testament.* 2nd ed. Downers Grove, IL: IVP Academic, 2014.

Klein, William W. *The New Chosen People: A Corporate View of Election.* 2nd ed. Eugene, OR: Wipf & Stock, 2015.

Lewis, C. S. *The Problem of Pain.* New York: HarperOne, 1940.

———. *Surprised by Joy.* San Francisco: HarperCollins, 1955.

MacDonald, Gregory. *The Evangelical Universalist.* 2nd ed. Eugene, OR: Wipf & Stock, 2012.

McClymond, Michael James. *The Devil's Redemption: A New History and Interpretation of Christian Universalism.* Grand Rapids: Baker Academic, 2018.

Packer, J. I. "Evangelicals and the Way of Salvation." In *Evangelical Affirmations*, edited by Kenneth S. Kantzer and Carl F. H. Henry, 107–36. Grand Rapids: Zondervan, 1990.

———. "Introductory Essay." In *The Death of Death in the Death of Christ*, by John Owen, 1–25. London: Banner of Truth, 1959.

Parry, Robin A. "A Universalist Response." In *Four Views on Hell*, edited by Preston M. Sprinkle, 89–94. 2nd ed. Grand Rapids: Zondervan, 2016.

———. "A Universalist View." In *Four Views on Hell*, edited by Preston M. Sprinkle, 101–27. 2nd ed. Grand Rapids: Zondervan, 2016.

Parry, Robin A., with Ilaria E. Ramelli. *A Larger Hope? Universal Salvation from the Reformation to the Nineteenth Century*. Eugene, OR: Cascade, 2019.

Parton, Curt. "Should Christians Obey the Ten Commandments? Christians and the Old Testament Law." *Exploring the Faith Archive* (blog), Jan. 19, 2012. https://exploringthefaitharchive.wordpress.com/2012/01/19/old-testament-law/.

Ramelli, Ilaria L. E. *The Christian Doctrine of Apokatastasis: A Critical Assessment from the New Testament to Eriugena*. Leiden: Brill Academic, 2013.

———. *A Larger Hope? Universal Salvation from Christian Beginnings to Julian of Norwich*. Eugene, OR: Cascade, 2019.

Ramelli, Ilaria, and David Konstan. *Terms for Eternity: Aiônios and Aïdios in Classical and Christian Texts*. Piscataway, NJ: Gorgias, 2013.

Sprinkle, Preston M. "Introduction." In *Four Views on Hell*, edited by Preston M. Sprinkle, 9–15. 2nd ed. Grand Rapids: Zondervan, 2016.

Stackhouse, John G., Jr. "Terminal Punishment." In *Four Views on Hell*, edited by Preston M. Sprinkle, 61–81. 2nd ed. Grand Rapids: Zondervan, 2016.

———. "A Terminal Punishment Response." In *Four Views on Hell*, edited by Preston M. Sprinkle, 44–47. 2nd ed. Grand Rapids: Zondervan, 2016.

Stott, John, and David L. Edwards. *Evangelical Essentials: A Liberal-Evangelical Dialogue*. Downers Grove, IL: InterVarsity, 1988.

Strand, Greg. "Eternal Conscious Punishment." *Strands of Thought* (blog), Aug. 11, 2015. https://blogs.efca.org/strands-of-thought/posts/eternal-conscious-punishment.

Talbott, Thomas B. *The Inescapable Love of God*. 2nd ed. Eugene, OR: Cascade, 2014.

Walls, Jerry L. "A Hell and Purgatory Response." In *Four Views on Hell*, edited by Preston M. Sprinkle, 140–44. 2nd ed. Grand Rapids: Zondervan, 2016.

———. *Hell: The Logic of Damnation*. Notre Dame: University of Notre Dame Press, 1992.

www.ingramcontent.com/pod-product-compliance
Lightning Source LLC
Chambersburg PA
CBHW060344100426
42812CB00003B/1115